Top Tips from the Baby Whisperer: Sleep

Secrets to Getting Your Baby
to Sleep through the Night

Tracy Hogg
with Melinda Blau

7 9 10 8

Published in 2009 by Vermilion, an imprint of Ebury Publishing

Ebury Publishing is a Random House Group company

The Random House Group Limited Reg. No. 954009

Addresses for companies within the Random House Group can be found at
www.randomhouse.co.uk

The Random House Group Limited supports The Forest Stewardship Council (FSC®), the leading
international forest certification organisation. Our books carrying the FSC label are printed on FSC®
certified paper. FSC is the only forest certification scheme endorsed by the leading environmental
organisations, including Greenpeace. Our paper procurement policy can be found at
www.randomhouse.co.uk/environment

Printed and bound in Great Britain by CPI Group (UK) Ltd, Croydon, CR0 4YY

ISBN 9780091929725

Text previously published in *The Baby Whisperer Solves All Your Problems*

Copies are available at special rates for bulk orders. Contact the sales development team
on 020 7840 8487 for more information.

To buy books by your favourite authors and register for offers, visit www.rbooks.co.uk

Contents

Introduction

I have always been proud of my ability to help parents understand and care for their young children and feel honoured whenever a family asks me into its life. During this time, on my website and in my email inbox, I've been inundated with requests for help, often on the subject of sleep. Maybe you're trying to get your baby on a structured routine to teach him to sleep better, or maybe your toddler is beginning to have sleep problems, but you're not sure what to do or even if the same principles apply to eight-month-olds as to newborns. When parents come to me with a particular challenge, I always ask at least one, if not a string of questions, both about the child and about what parents have done so far in response to their situation. Then I can come up with a proper plan of action. My goal is to help you understand my thought process and get you in the habit of asking questions for yourself.

Tuning In

Baby whispering begins by observing, respecting and communicating with your baby – observing body language, listening to cries, slowing down so that you can really figure out what's going on. It means that you see your child's personality and particular quirks – and you tailor your parenting strategies accordingly.

'Why doesn't it work?' is by far one of the most common questions parents ask. Whether a mum is trying to get her infant to sleep more than two hours at a time or her toddler to nap properly, I often hear the old 'yes, but' response. 'Yes, I know you told me I have to wake her during the day in order for her to sleep at night, but . . .' 'Yes, I know you told me it will take time, but . . .'

Granted, I know that some babies are more challenging than others – just like adults – but my baby whispering techniques do work; I've used them myself with thousands of babies.

When problems persist, it's usually because of something the parents have done, so you need to ask yourself if one of the following statements applies to you:

You're following your child, rather than establishing a routine. I'm a firm believer in a structured routine (see chapter 1). You start, ideally, from the day you bring your little bundle home from the hospital. You could also introduce a routine later, but the older the baby, the more trouble parents often have.

You've been doing accidental parenting. Unfortunately, in the heat of the moment parents sometimes do *anything* to make their baby stop crying or to get a toddler to calm down. Often, the 'anything' – whether walking, rocking, jiggling – turns into a bad habit that they later have to break – and that's accidental parenting.

You're not reading your child's cues. 'He used to be on schedule, and now he's not. How do I get him back on track?' When I hear any version of that phrase – 'used to be and now is not' – it usually means they're paying more attention to the clock (or their own needs) than the baby himself.

You're not factoring in that young children change constantly. I also hear the 'used to be' phrase when parents don't realise that it's time to make a shift; the only constant in the job of parenting is change.

You're looking for an easy fix. The older a child is, the harder it is to break a bad habit caused by accidental parenting. Be patient.

You're not really committed to change. If you're trying to solve a problem, you have to want it solved – and have the determination and stamina to see it through to the end. If we stick with it, children do get used to the new way.

Parents sometimes delude themselves. They will insist that they've been trying a particular technique for two weeks and say it's not working. Often they've tried for three or four days, and it worked, but a few days later they didn't follow through with the original plan. The poor child is then confused.

If you're not going to see something through, don't do it. If you can't do it on your own, enlist backup people.

You're trying something that doesn't work for your family or your personality. If you're not comfortable doing a particular technique, either don't do it, or find ways to bolster yourself, by having the stronger parent take over for a bit, or enlisting a relative or a good friend to help.

It ain't broke – and you don't really need to fix it. Babies are individuals. Your baby may be sleeping less than another baby or have a smaller-than-average build. If it isn't a concern to your doctor, just observe your child.

You have unrealistic expectations. Babies *do* sometimes need to feed in the night. Children require care, constant vigilance and lots of loving time.

I'm not a big fan of age charts and never have been. Babies' challenges can't be sorted into neat piles. Still, I have broken down my advice and tailored various techniques according to age groupings to give you a better understanding of how your child thinks and sees the world. I urge you to read all the stages, because earlier problems can persist, or your child might be more advanced in a particular area.

Where We Go from Here

You can read this book cover to cover, or just look up the problems you're concerned about and go from there. However, I strongly recommend that you at least read through chapter 1, which reviews my basic philosophy of a structured routine for your child. Throughout, I've tried to zero in on the most common concerns that parents have when it comes to their child and sleep, and then share with you the kinds of questions I typically ask to find out what's really going on (when I've reprinted emails and website postings, names and identifying details have been changed) and what I would suggest to deal with these concerns. You might be surprised by some of these, but I have lots of examples to demonstrate how successfully they've been applied in other families. So why not at least try them with yours?

CHAPTER ONE

E.A.S.Y. Isn't Necessarily Easy (But It Works!)

Getting Your Baby on a Structured Routine

The Gift of E.A.S.Y.

You probably have a routine in the morning. You get up at roughly the same time, maybe you shower first or have your coffee, or perhaps you take your dog out for a brisk walk. Whatever you do, it's probably pretty much the same every morning. If by chance something interrupts that routine, it can throw off your whole day. Human beings thrive when they know how and when their needs are going to be met and what's coming next.

Well, that includes babies and young children. When a new mum brings her baby home from the hospital, I suggest a structured routine straightaway. I call it 'E.A.S.Y.', an acronym that stands for a predictable sequence of events that pretty much mirrors how adults live their lives, albeit in shorter chunks: **E**at, have some **A**ctivity (so the little one doesn't associate eating with sleeping) and go to **S**leep, which leaves a bit of time for **Y**ou. It is *not* a schedule, because you cannot fit a baby into a clock. It's a routine that gives the day structure and makes family life consistent.

With E.A.S.Y., you don't follow the baby; you observe him carefully, tune in to his cues, but you take the lead, gently encouraging him to follow what you know will make him thrive. The acronym is simply designed to help parents remember the order of the routine.

Eating affects sleep and activity; activity affects eating and sleeping; sleep affects activity and eating – changes in one usually affect the other two. Although your baby will transform over the coming months as she grows, the order in which each letter occurs does not:

E*at*. Your baby's day starts with a feed, which goes from all-liquid to liquids and solids at six months. You're less likely to overfeed or underfeed a baby who's on a routine.

A*ctivity*. Infants entertain themselves by staring at the

wallpaper. But as your baby develops she will interact more with her environment and move about. A structured routine helps prevent babies from becoming overstimulated.

S*leep*. Sleep helps your baby grow. And good naps during the day will make her go for longer stretches at night, because she needs to be relaxed in order to sleep well.

Y*our time*. If every day is different and unpredictable, your baby will be miserable – and you'll barely have a moment for yourself.

Write It Down!

Parents who actually chart their baby's day *by writing everything down* have less trouble sticking to a routine or establishing it for the first time. They will also find patterns more obvious – it will be clearer how sleep and eating and activity are interrelated.

E.A.S.Y. isn't necessarily easy. Some babies will adapt more rapidly and readily than others because of their basic temperament. And some special birth conditions (like prematurity or jaundice) or a particular infant's weight mean that E.A.S.Y. needs to be adapted. Also, some parents misunderstand how to apply E.A.S.Y. For instance, they take 'every three hours' literally and wonder what kind of activity should be done after a feed in the middle of the night. (None – you send him right back to sleep.)

A *structured routine* is not the same thing as a schedule. A schedule is about time slots whereas E.A.S.Y. is about keeping up the same daily pattern – eating, activity and sleeping – and repeating that pattern every day. If you're busy watching the clock, instead of your baby, you'll miss important signals (like the first signs of tiredness). So if one day he seems tired before it's 'time' to put him down, don't let the clock threaten you. Let your common sense take over.

Guidelines to Get You Started

The E.A.S.Y. Log

When parents come home from the hospital and start E.A.S.Y., I usually suggest that they keep a log, so that they keep track of exactly what their baby is eating and doing, how long she's sleeping, and also what the mum is doing for herself.

Guidelines for Different Ages

Establishing a routine for the first time gets a bit harder as the baby grows, especially if you've never had structure. So, no matter how old your baby is, it's a good idea to read through all the sections, because, as I will remind you repeatedly, *you can't base strategies solely on age.*

The first six weeks: adjustment time

The first six weeks is the ideal time to start E.A.S.Y., which generally starts out as a three-hour plan. Your baby eats, plays after his feeds, you then set the scene for good napping. You rest while he rests, and when he wakes up, the cycle starts again.

The average baby cries somewhere between one and five hours out of 24 and we should never ignore a baby's cries or, in my opinion, let him cry it out! Instead, we always have to try to figure out what he's telling us. It's understandable, but when the parents of young infants have problems with

E.A.S.Y. it's usually because they're misreading their baby's cries, confusing a hungry cry with an overtired cry, for example.

The crying questions
When a six-week or younger baby cries, it's always easier to determine what she wants if you know where she is in her day. Ask yourself:

Is it time for a feed? (hunger)

Is her nappy wet or soiled? (discomfort or cold)

Has she been sitting in the same place or position without a change of scene? (boredom)

Has she been up for more than 30 minutes? (overtired)

Has she had lots of company or has there been a lot of activity in your household? (overstimulated)

Is she grimacing and pulling her legs up? (wind)

Is she crying inconsolably during or as much as an hour after feeds? (reflux)

Is she spitting up? (reflux)

Is the room too hot or cold, or is she under- or overdressed? (body temperature)

A Typical E.A.S.Y. Day for a 4-Week-Old

E	7.00	Feed.
A	7.45	Nappy change; some playing and talking; watch cues for sleepiness.
S	8.15	Swaddle and lay your baby in the cot. It may take him 15–20 minutes to fall asleep for his 1st morning nap.
Y	8.30	You nap when he naps.
E	10.00	Feed.
A	10.45	See 7.45 above.
S	11.15	2nd morning nap.
Y	11.30	You nap or at least relax.
E	1.00	Feed.
A	1.45	See 7.45 above.

A Typical E.A.S.Y. Day for a 4-Week-Old (cont'd)

S	2.15	Afternoon nap.
Y	2.30	You nap or at least relax.
E	4.00	Feed.
A	4.45	See 7.45 above.
S	5.15	Catnap for 40–50 minutes to give him enough rest to handle his bath.
Y	5.30	Do something nice for yourself.
E	6.00	1st cluster feed (increasing your baby's intake in the early evening to help his sleep).
A	7.00	Bath, into night clothes, lullaby or other bedtime ritual.
S	7.30	Another catnap.
Y	7.30	You eat dinner.
E	8.00	2nd cluster feed.
A		None.
S		Put him right back to bed.
Y		Enjoy your short evening!
E	10-11	Dream feed (literally feeding your baby in his sleep; at the end of the dream feed, your baby will be so relaxed you can put him down without burping) and cross your fingers until morning!

Note: Whether a baby is breast- or bottle-fed, I advise the above routine – allowing for variations in times – until four months old. The 'A' time will be shorter for younger babies, and get progressively longer for older ones. I also recommend turning the two 'cluster feeds' into one (at around 5.30 or 6) by eight weeks. Continue the dream feed until seven months – unless he's a great sleeper and makes it through on his own.

Common complaints and probable causes

Complaint: I can't get my baby to conform to a three-hour routine. I can't get her to do even 20 minutes of activity time.

Cause: If your baby weighs less than 3 kg (6½ pounds) at birth, she may need to eat every two hours at first (see 'E.A.S.Y. by Weight' page 17). Don't try to keep her awake for activities.

Complaint: My baby often falls asleep during feeds and seems hungry an hour later.

Cause: This is common to premature, jaundiced, low-birthweight and some simply sleepy babies. You might have to feed more often and definitely have to work at keeping him awake for his feeds. If breastfed, the cause could be improper latch-on, or mum's milk supply.

Complaint: My baby wants to eat every two hours.
Cause: If your baby weighs 3 kg (6½ pounds) or more, he may not be eating efficiently. Watch out that he doesn't turn into a 'snacker'. If breastfed, the cause could be improper latch-on, or mum's milk supply.

Complaint: My baby is rooting all the time and I keep thinking he's hungry, but he only takes a little bit at each feed.
Cause: Your baby may not be getting enough suckling time, so he's using the bottle or breast as a pacifier. He may be turning into a 'snacker'. Check your milk supply by doing a yield.

Complaint: My baby doesn't take regular naps.
Cause: He may be overstimulated by too much activity. Or you are not persevering with swaddling him and laying him down awake.

Complaint: My baby is a great napper, but she's up frequently
at night.

Cause: Your baby has switched night for day and her
daytime sleep is robbing her night-time sleep.

Complaint: I never know what my baby wants when he's
crying.

Cause: Your baby may have a touchy or grumpy temperament or have a physical problem, such as
wind, reflux or colic. Whatever the cause, you and
he will do better if he's on E.A.S.Y.

E.A.S.Y. by Weight

E.A.S.Y. was designed for an average-weight newborn – 3–3.5
kg (6½–8 pounds) – babies who generally can last three hours
between feeds. If your baby weighs more or less, you will have
to adjust. The following chart shows how birthweight affects
your baby's routine. (After four months, even most low-weight
babies can last four hours between feeds.) Note the time your
baby usually wakes up, and write down approximate times based
on your baby's weight and the information in the 'how often'
column. Allow for variation – it's not the time slot that matters

as much as predictability and order. To simplify, I've left out the 'Y'-time for You. If your baby weighs less than 3 kg (6½ pounds), you won't have much time for yourself, especially in the first six weeks. But hang in there – this phase will get better.

Weight	2.25–3 kg (5–6½ pounds)		3–3.5 kg (6½–8 pounds)		Over 3.5 kg (8 pounds)	
	How long	**How often**	**How long**	**How often**	**How long**	**How often**
Eat	30–40 minutes	Routine repeats every 2 hours during the day, until baby weighs 3 kg (6½ lb), at which point you can switch to an every-3-hour plan. At first these babies can only go 4 hours at night without eating.	25–40 minutes	Routine repeats every 2½–3 hours (for babies on the lower end of average) during the day; 4- to 5-hour stretches at night in the first 6 weeks, by which time you should be working at cutting out the 1 or 2am feed.	25–35 minutes	Routine repeats every 3 hours during the day. By 6 weeks, these babies can generally cut out the 1 or 2am feed and will do a 5- or 6-hour stretch from 11 to 4 or 5am.
Activity	5–10 minutes at first; 20 minutes at 3 kg (6½ lb), gradually extend time to 45 minutes when they are around 3.25 kg (7 lb).		20–45 minutes (includes nappy changing, dressing and, once a day, a bath).		20–45 minutes (includes nappy changing, dressing and, once a day, a bath).	
Sleep	1¼–1½ hours		1½–2 hours		1½–2 hours	

Six weeks to four months: unexpected wake-ups

Compared to the first six weeks at home – the classic post-partum period – during the next two and a half months or so, everyone starts to be on a more even keel. You're more confident, and, we hope, a little less harried.

Common complaints and probable causes

Complaint: I can't get my baby to sleep more than three or four hours during the night.

Cause: She may not be getting enough food during the day, and you also might need to 'tank her up' before bedtime.

Complaint: My baby was sleeping for five or six hours during the night, but now she's waking up more frequently, but always at different times.

Cause: Your baby is probably having a growth spurt and needs more food during the day.

Complaint: I can't get my baby to nap for more than half an hour or 45 minutes.

Cause: You're probably either not getting him to bed when he first shows signs of fatigue, or you're going in too soon when he first stirs, which doesn't give him a chance to go back to sleep on his own.

Complaint: My baby wakes up at the same hour every night but never takes more than a few ml/ounces when I try to feed him.

Cause: Habitual waking is almost never about hunger. Your baby is probably waking out of habit.

As you can see, the problem that usually presents in babies this age is a sudden, inexplicable (to the parents, at least) departure from the 'S' part of their routine. Some night waking is naturally due to hunger but that's not always the case. Depending on what the parents do in response to their baby's night waking and nap problems, their well-intentioned actions can lay the seeds of accidental parenting. Say your baby awoke one night and you calmed her by giving her your breast or a bottle. It worked like a charm, but you're inadvertently teaching her that she needs to suckle in order to get back to sleep. Believe me, when she is six months old, you're going to regret that quick fix.

Four to six months: '4/4' and the beginnings of accidental parenting

At this stage, your baby can hold up her head easily and is beginning to grasp at things. She is learning to, or already can, roll over. She can sit up fairly straight with your help, so her perspective is changing, too. She's more aware of patterns and routine. She has grown increasingly better at distinguishing where sounds come from and figuring out cause and effect; she has a better memory, too.

Because of these strides in development, your baby's daily routine naturally has to change, too – hence, my '4/4' rule of thumb, which stands for 'four months/four-hour E.A.S.Y.'. Most babies are ready at this point to switch from a three- to four-hour routine. You can cut one feed because she's taking in more at each feed, consolidate three naps into two naps (keeping the late afternoon catnap in either case), and thereby extend your baby's waking hours.

Comparing the three-hour and four-hour routines

3-hour E.A.S.Y.	4-hour E.A.S.Y.
E: 7.00 Wake up and feed	E: 7.00 Wake up and feed
A: 7.30 or 7.45 (depending on how long feed takes)	A: 7.30
S: 8.30 (1½ hour nap)	S: 9.00 (1½–2 hour nap)
Y: Your choice	Y: Your choice
E: 10.00	E: 11.00
A: 10.30 or 10.45	A: 11.30
S: 11.30 (1½ hour nap)	S: 1.00 (1½–2 hour)
Y: Your choice	Y: Your choice
E: 1.00	E: 3.00
A: 1.30 or 1.45	A: 3.30
S: 2.30 (1½ hour nap)	S: 5.00 or 6.00 or somewhere in between: Catnap
Y: Your choice	Y: Your choice
E: 4.00 feed	E: 7.00 (cluster feed at 7.00 and 9.00, only if going through a growth spurt)
S: 5.00 or 6.00 or somewhere in between: Catnap (approximately 40 minutes) to get Baby through the next feed and bath	A: Bath
	S: 7.30 Bedtime
	Y: The evening is yours!

E: 7.00 (cluster feed at 7.00 and 9.00 if going through a growth spurt) **A:** Bath **S:** 7.30 Bedtime **Y:** The evening is yours! **E:** 10.00 or 11.00 Dream feed	**E:** 11.00 Dream feed (until 7 or 8 months, or whenever solid food is firmly established)

Your baby won't necessarily conform exactly to these times. Your child might even veer from her own schedule 15 minutes here and there. One day she'll have a shorter nap in the morning and a longer one in the afternoon, or she'll alternate between the two. The important consideration is that you stick to the eat/activity/sleep pattern (now at four-hour intervals).

Common complaints and probable causes

Complaint: My baby finishes her feeds so quickly, I'm afraid she's not getting enough to eat. It also throws off her routine.

Cause: The E may not be a problem at all – some babies are quite efficient eaters by now. You may be trying to keep your child on an E.A.S.Y. plan meant for a younger child – every three hours instead of four.

Complaint: My baby never eats or sleeps at the same time.
Cause: Some variation in your daily routine is normal. But if he's snacking and catnapping – both the result of accidental parenting – he's never getting a good meal or a good sleep. He needs to be on a structured routine suitable for a four-month-old.

Complaint: My baby is still waking up frequently every night, and I never know whether or not to feed him.
Cause: If it's erratic waking, he's hungry and needs more food during the day; if it's habitual waking, you have accidentally reinforced a bad habit. You also might have him on a three- instead of four-hour routine.

Complaint: My baby makes it through the night but wakes up at five and wants to play.
Cause: You might be responding too early to his normal early morning sounds and have inadvertently taught him that it's a good idea to wake up so early.

Complaint: I can't get my baby to nap for more than half an hour or 45 minutes – or she refuses to nap at all.

Cause: She may be overstimulated before naptime, or this is the result of a lack of, or improper, routine – or both.

Six to nine months: riding out the inconsistencies

We're still looking at a four-hour routine at this stage but, by six months, there's a major growth spurt, too. It's the prime time to introduce solid food, and, by seven months or so, to cut out the dream feed.

Mealtimes are a little longer – and a lot messier – as your baby gets to try a whole new way of eating. Now, too, the early evening catnap disappears, and most babies are down to two naps a day – ideally, each one lasting one to two hours. Napping is not a favourite pastime of babies at this stage, physical development now takes centre stage, by eight months your baby can hold himself upright, he is becoming more coordinated and he'll be a lot more independent.

The common complaints at this stage are pretty much the same as we saw at four to six months – except, of course, habits are more deeply entrenched and will take a little longer to solve.

Otherwise, the biggest issue that crops up at this point is inconsistency. Some days your baby will take a long nap in the morning, other days it happens in the afternoon, and still other days he might drop one of his naps altogether. The key to survival is twofold: if he doesn't stick to a routine, at least you can.

The fact is, because babies nine months and older can stay up for longer stretches without sleeping, it is possible for them to start skipping the morning nap altogether and take one long nap in the afternoon – for as long as three hours. They eat, play, eat again, play some more and then go to sleep. In other words, 'E.AS.Y.' becomes 'E.A.E.A.S.Y.'

Starting E.A.S.Y. at four months or older

If your baby is four months or older, and she's never had a routine, it's time to put her on one. The process is different from that of younger babies for three important reasons:

1. *It's a four-hour routine.* It's important that parents realise they have to adjust the routine to their child's more advanced development.

2. *We use my 'pick-up/put-down method' (P.U./P.D.) to make changes.* With babies over four months old, sleep difficulties are invariably part of the reason why it's

impossible to sustain a daily routine. P.U./P.D. can help deal with this (see chapter 3).

3. *Establishing a structured routine over four months is almost always complicated by accidental parenting.* Because most parents have already tried other methods, or a medley of methods, the baby has already got into a bad habit. Therefore, putting an older baby on E.A.S.Y. invariably involves more commitment and work – and consistency.

Making time for change

The thing to keep in mind when introducing a routine for the first time is that there are rarely overnight miracles – three days, a week, even two, but never overnight. When ushering in any new regime to a baby of any age, you're going to get resistance. The good news is that, if you're as consistent with the new way as you have been with the old, he'll eventually get used to it.

> **It's a Myth:**
> Catnaps Ruin Sleep
>
> Many babies between four and six months take a 30- to 40-minute catnap in the late afternoon, even as late as 5. Parents worry that the extra nap will ruin night-time sleep. It's just the opposite: the more rest your baby gets in the day, the better she will sleep at night.

CHAPTER TWO
Teaching Babies How to Sleep

The First Three Months and the Six Troubleshooting Variables

Sleep is the Number One issue that plagues parents from the moment they bring their baby home from the hospital: if you have a tired child, he won't eat or play; he'll be cranky, and prone to digestive problems and other illnesses. Even the lucky ones, whose babies are naturally good sleepers, wonder, 'When will my baby sleep through the night?'

In almost every case of sleep difficulties, parents have the same basic problem: they don't realise that sleep is a set of skills that we have to *teach* babies – how to fall asleep on their own and, when they wake in the middle of the night, how to get back to sleep. And instead of taking the lead in those first three months when they should be laying the groundwork for good sleep habits, they follow the baby and, without realising it, allow all sorts of bad habits to develop.

Just like adults, babies go through 45-minute cycles, alternating a deep, almost coma-like sleep with lighter REM (rapid eye movement), when the brain is active and we tend to dream. Research proves that, on average, babies actually spend 50 to 66 per cent of their sleep time in REM, far more than adults, who average 15 to 20 per cent. Thus, babies often wake up throughout the night, just as we do.

The Six Troubleshooting Variables

Sleep problems at any age tend to have multiple causes. Also, a sleep 'problem' tonight might not have the same cause as last night's. Your baby could wake up because the room is too cold one night, because he's hungry the next, and because he's in pain a few nights later.

Making the picture even more complex, the phrase 'sleeping through the night' confuses many parents. The mother of an eight-week-old wrote to me: 'I want him to be asleep by 7 – and to get up at 7. What do you suggest?' I suggest *Mum* needs help, not her child. Let's be realistic: babies don't actually sleep *through the night* in the early months. In the first six weeks, most wake twice a night – at 2 or 3am and then at 5 or 6am – because their stomachs can't hold enough to sustain them longer than that. They also need the calories to grow. We work towards getting rid of that 2am feed first. You probably won't reach that goal until your baby is four to six weeks at best, depending on your baby's temperament and size among other factors and, even when your baby is over six weeks and is able to sleep through a longer stretch, you might still be getting up at 4 or 5 or 6 in the morning at first.

I've isolated six different variables that can affect sleep during the first three months. All six variables are related and sometimes intertwined and can continue to affect your baby's sleep habits well past the four-month mark, into the toddler years, and, sadly, even beyond. These Six Troubleshooting Variables are:

Don't Do It Alone!

Sleep deprivation is a parent's problem, not a baby's. Especially in the first six weeks, get lots of help. Trade off with your partner to make sure the burden of middle-of-the-night feeds doesn't only fall on your shoulders, but not every other night; each should be 'on duty' for two nights and off for two, so that you can really catch up on your sleep. If you're a single mum, ask your own mother or a good friend to pitch in. If no one can sleep over, at least invite them to come a few hours during the day to give you a chance to sleep.

The parents might have
  1. failed to establish a daily routine
  2. set up an inadequate sleep ritual
  3. got into accidental parenting

The child might be
  4. hungry
  5. overstimulated or overtired, or both
  6. in pain, uncomfortable or ill

Especially in the middle of the night when adults are at their worst, it's not a simple matter to figure out which of the variables is the culprit – even more so, if there's more than one at work! But work at it to find the clues to the cause – or causes – and a plan. Each of six variables, below, includes a list of 'tip-offs' – most of the tip-offs are listed in more than one variable, so it's important to read through and understand each of them.

Variable Number 1: Lack of Routine

Tip-offs

• My baby doesn't settle down to sleep easily

- My baby wakes up every hour at night
- My baby sleeps well during the day but is up all night

Do you keep track of his feeds, naps, bedtimes and wake-up times? If the answer is no, I suspect that the parents have never established a structured routine or they've been unable to stick to one.

No routine. Sensible sleep is the 'S' in E.A.S.Y. And in the first three months, it's often mainly about trying to keep your baby on E.A.S.Y. For average-birthweight babies under four months of age, staying on a three-hour routine is an essential key to success.

A PLAN: If you're not on a structured routine, commit to giving your baby a predictable sequence of events. Or re-establish E.A.S.Y. if you've got off track. Include my 'Four S' wind-down ritual (see pages 38–42) every time you put him down.

The day-for-night dilemma. When a baby is born, she's on a 24-hour clock and doesn't know the difference between day and night. We have to teach her to do that (typically at eight weeks or younger) by waking her for her regular feeds and being consistent with the daytime routine. **How many naps a**

day does she take, and for how long? How much daytime sleep is she getting altogether? More than five and a half hours of sleep during the day will throw the three-hour routine off kilter and cause a baby to stay up all night.

A PLAN: If your baby sleeps more than two hours during the day, wake her. If you don't and you allow her to sleep through a feed, she's going to have to make up for the lost nutrition at night. You may have been told never to wake a sleeping baby, but that's a myth. Waking a baby is not only acceptable, it's imperative at times, because in the end it enables her to get on a structured routine.

Don't allow your baby to sleep longer than 45 minutes to an hour during the day for the first three days. This will get her out of the long-nap habit and ensure that she gets the calories she needs by regular feeds. To wake her, unswaddle her, pick her up, massage her little hands and take her into an area where there's activity. Sit her upright, a simple trick which should make her eyes pop open. Once you've reduced her daytime sleep, your baby will start making up the hours at night and you can gradually – every three days – increase her naptime by 15 minutes. Never let her sleep for more than one and a half to two hours during the day, which is the proper nap period for babies four months and younger.

Routine busters. **Do you schlepp your baby with you on errands throughout the day?** Sometimes parents veer from their routine with a young baby because of their own needs. It's important to keep to your routine during the early months; consistency is vital.

A PLAN: I'm not saying that you shouldn't ever leave the house. But if your baby is having trouble settling down, it might be because she's not able to go with your flow. For at least two weeks, commit to a structured routine, observe her cues, and establish a good sleep ritual. **Even though you have a good routine, if you work full- or part-time, do you know that whoever else is taking care of your child – your partner, Grandma, a nanny, or a day care provider – is following it, too?** If you have a nanny, stay at

Premature and small babies

The only exception to cutting back naptime is a premature or small baby. If your baby was premature, his chrono-logical age – from the day he was born – is not the same as his developmental age. Some small babies take five half-hour naps during the day at first, have only a few minutes of up time in between, and fall asleep until the next feed. You just have to ride it out for a few weeks. He will be on a two-hour routine, at least until he reaches your due date. When he reaches or is past his due date and weighs at least 3 kg (6½ pounds), you can extend his awake time during the day and put him on a three-hour routine.

home for a week to show her your routine, including your wind-down ritual. If you take your child to a day care provider away from home, spend extra time there to show the person or staff how you handle your baby and what you do at naptimes.

Variable Number 2: Inadequate Sleep Ritual

Tip-offs

- My baby doesn't settle down to sleep easily
- My baby falls asleep but then is suddenly awake, 10 minutes to half an hour later

'Going to sleep' is not a single event. It begins with your baby's first yawn and ends with her finally dropping off into a deep sleep. You have to help her get there by recognising her sleep window and helping her wind down.

The sleep window. **Do you know what your baby looks like when she's tired? Do you act on it immediately?** If you miss your baby's sleep window, it's going to be a lot harder to get her to sleep.

A PLAN: Some infants are naturally better sleepers than others – but all babies need their parents to be observant (it often helps to create a sleep diary over four days). With newborns a yawn is often the biggest clue. But your baby might also fuss, fidget, or make other involuntary movements. Some open their eyes wide while others sound like a creaking door and still others squeak. By six weeks, he might also turn away from your face or from a toy, or burrow into your neck when you're carrying him. Whatever his particular signs, *act immediately*. If you miss your baby's sleep window, or try to extend his awake time in the name of getting him to sleep longer (another myth), it's going to be a lot harder to teach him the skills of settling down.

Winding down. Even if you recognise when your baby is tired, you can't just plop her straight into her cot without giving her a few moments to transition from an activity. **What method have you been using to put her to bed or down for a nap? Do you swaddle her?** If she has trouble settling in, do you stay with her? A wind-down ritual – a predictable, repetitive sequence – allows a baby to learn what to expect, and swaddling helps a baby feel cosy and safe. Both act like cues, in essence telling your baby, 'It's time to switch gears. We're getting ready for sleep.' This need not take too long (with a child under three months old, generally no longer than 15 minutes), but starting a wind-down ritual when your baby is very young will not only teach the sleep skills she needs, it will also lay a foundation of trust for when separation anxiety kicks in.

A PLAN: My 'Four S' ritual consists of *Setting the stage* (getting the environment ready for sleep), *Swaddling* (getting your baby ready for sleep), *Sitting* (quietly, without physical stimulation) and, when necessary, doing the *Shush-pat* method (spending an extra few minutes of physical intervention to help a fussy or fidgety baby drop off into a deep sleep).

Setting the stage. Whether it's bedtime or naptime, you set the stage for sleep by removing your baby from a stimulating setting to a more calm one. Go into the room, draw the curtains and, if you like, put on soft music.

Swaddling. Under the age of three months, babies have no control over their limbs – their arms and legs jerk or wave in the air when they're exhausted. And when that happens, the baby doesn't even realise that her limbs are attached to her – they distract and disturb her. The hospital will probably have swaddled your baby, and shown you how to do it, and I recommend swaddling at least up to three or four months (when they start to find their fingers), although some babies can go as long as seven or eight months. Some parents are fearful of wrapping their baby lest it restrict his breathing or his leg movements, but research has shown that proper swaddling doesn't put infants at risk and actually helps babies sleep more soundly.

At a certain point in her development, your baby's arms will come out of the swaddling and she will start to explore and move around. Some babies do this as early as four weeks. If your baby gets out of her swaddle, reswaddle her. Later, at around four months, you might choose to experiment by leaving one arm out of the swaddle so that she can work at finding her fist or fingers.

Sitting. After your baby is swaddled, quietly sit with him in the vertical position for around five minutes. With a young baby it's best to hold him so that his face is tucked into your neck or shoulder, to block out any visual stimulation. Don't rock or jiggle him, and don't pace – this will stimulate him rather than calm him. You should feel his little body relax and then maybe jerk a little. That's him trying to descend into a deep sleep. Ideally, you want to put your baby into his cot before he sleeps (infants and toddlers who are put to bed awake are more likely to sleep longer hours than babies who are put to bed asleep, and are less likely to wake two or three times during the night). As you're about to lay him down, say, 'You're going to sleep now. I'll see you when you get up.' Give him a kiss, and then put him in his cot. If he seems calm, leave the room and allow him to drift off to sleep on his own. Unless he's having problems settling down, *you don't have to wait for him to fall asleep.*

Shush-pat. If your baby is a bit fussy, or he starts crying when you try to lay him down, he is probably ready for sleep but needs physical intervention in order to settle. This is the point at which parents rock or jiggle or use some kind of prop to calm their baby. But my suggestion (for babies under the age of three months) is the shush-pat method: you simultaneously whisper 'shh, shh, shh . . .' into your baby's ear and pat his back. At this point in their development, they can't continue to concentrate on the crying while being patted and shushed, so your baby will focus instead on the shush and the pat, and eventually stop crying. But it's critical that you do the shush-pat as follows:

- Pat him on the centre of his back (not on one side or the other, and certainly not as far down as his kidneys) in a steady, rhythmic motion – like the tick-tock of a clock. The patting needs to be quite firm, and you should do this while he's lying in the cot or, if that doesn't settle him, hold him over your shoulder.

- While you're patting him, put your mouth near his ear, and whisper a slow, fairly loud, 'Shh . . . shh . . . shh.' Elongate the *shh* sound, so that it comes out more like the whooshing of air not the slow chug-chug of a train. (The shushing should go *past* his ear, not directly into his ear, because you don't want to perforate his eardrum.)

- When you sense that his breathing is getting a little deeper and his body is starting to relax, gently lay him down, slightly on his side, so that you can have access to his back. If he's swaddled, use a wedge or rolled-up towel to keep him in place. I also like to put my other hand on the chest, and then pat on the back. Then you can also bend down to his ear and do the shushing without picking him up. If the room isn't dark enough, you might also have to put your hand over (not on) his eyes to block out visual stimulation.

- I pat probably seven to ten minutes after the baby has calmed down. Even if he's quiet, I don't stop until I'm fairly sure he has his complete focus on it, and then I start to slow the patting down more and more. Finally, I also stop the shush. Continue the shush-pat until he settles. If he cries, pick him up again, and do the shush-pat with him on your shoulder. When you put him down again, continue to pat him and see if he starts up again. If he does, pick him up and calm him down *again*.

- When he's quiet, gently lay him on his back, step back from the cot and stay a few minutes to see whether he falls into a deep sleep or jolts again to consciousness as some babies do.

Remember that it takes a baby 20 minutes to pass through the three stages of sleep – *the window* (the point at which you notice his sleep cues and set the scene), *the zone* (when he gets a glazed look in his eye, by which time you've swaddled him), and the *letting go* (he starts to nod off). The letting-go stage is the trickiest – often your baby's eyes shut, you stop patting and sneak out of the room, but then his whole body jolts and his eyes pop open. When you leave too soon, you could be in and out every 10 minutes for an hour and a half. And each time, you have to start the process again, which can take a full 20 minutes.

You'll know your baby is in a deep sleep when his eyes stop moving side to side under his lids, his breathing slows and becomes more shallow, and his body completely relaxes, as if he's melting into the mattress.

Variable Number 3: Accidental Parenting

Tip-offs

- My baby won't sleep unless I … rock her, feed her, lay her on my chest, etc.
- My baby seems tired, but the minute I start to put her down, she cries
- My baby wakes up at the same time every night
- When my baby wakes at night, I feed her but she rarely takes much
- I can't get my baby to nap for more than half an hour or 45 minutes
- My baby wakes up at 5am to start her day
- My baby refuses to sleep in her own cot
- My baby wakes when the dummy drops out of her mouth

I have often stressed the importance of patient and conscious (P.C.) parenting; *accidental parenting* is the opposite.

Prop dependency. A 'prop' is *any* object or action outside of the baby's control that a parent employs to get a child to sleep. **Do you routinely hold, rock, walk or bounce your baby to** sleep? Breastfeed or give her a bottle to calm her down? **Allow her to fall asleep on your chest, in a swing or a car seat? Take her into your bed when she's upset?** If you answer 'yes' to any of the above, you're using a prop, and I promise it will come back to haunt you.

Often, prop dependency starts out as a desperate measure but, even if you employ a prop just for a few nights in a row, it will quickly get to the point where she can't settle down or drift off to sleep without it. And by the time she's three or four months old, if you don't keep up whatever prop you've got her used to, she'll cry to bring you back into the room to replace it.

A PLAN: Think through the practices you adopt. Will you want to be pacing or nursing when your baby is five months old? Eleven months old? Two? Will you want to take him into your bed in the middle of the night until he decides he doesn't need it any more? Better to avoid the props now than take them away later on, which is much harder.

If you've already fallen into the trap of using a prop, the good news is that bad habits fade quickly in these early months. Instead of relying on your prop, do the Four S ritual (pages 38–42). It may take three days, six days, even longer than a week, but, if you're consistent, you can wean him from the bad habit you created.

The perils of rushing in. A baby's sleep pattern, whether she wakes frequently and/or at the same time every night, often gives me important clues about where parents inadvertently go wrong. **How many times does she wake up during the night?** A newborn on a good routine should wake no more than twice a night. If your baby is waking up every hour, or even every two hours, and we've ruled out hunger and pain, there's a good chance that you are doing something that makes night-time appealing to her. **What do you do with her when she wakes up in the middle of the night or when she wakes up early from a nap? Do you rush in? Do you play with her? Take her into your bed?**

I don't believe in allowing a baby to cry. However, sometimes parents don't realise that stirring is not the

Props vs. Comfort Items

A prop is *not* the same as a comfort item: a prop is something *the parent* chooses and controls; a comfort item, like a blanket or favourite stuffed toy, is something *the child* adopts. Props are often given within the first few weeks of birth; babies don't adopt comfort items until six months or older.

Dummies can go either way: if the child always wakes when it falls out and needs a parent to put it back in, it's a prop. If the child stays asleep without it, or can pop it back in on his own, it's a comfort item.

same as waking. If you answered 'yes' to any of the above, you might be going into the room prematurely and actually disturbing her sleep, or cutting it short. Left to her own devices, she might fall asleep again. It's the same with early morning wake-ups.

A Plan: Listen, respond to cries, but don't rush in and rescue. Every baby makes little infant noises when they start to come out of a deep sleep; get to know what your baby sounds like. If you hear your baby in the middle of the night or during an afternoon nap, don't rush in. And when she wakes at 5 or 5.30, and you know (because she's on a good routine and you're monitoring her daytime feeds) that she's hungry, just feed her, swaddle her and then put her right back down at 5.30. Use the shush-pat if necessary. When you finally do go in later in the morning, watch your tone. Don't act as if this poor little thing has been abandoned by you.

Habitual waking. Just as adults tend to get into waking habits, so do babies. Some babies go back to sleep, but others cry out, and their parents come running. When they do, they inadvertently reinforce the habit. **Does she wake up at the same time every night?** If so, and if she wakes up more than two days in a row at that time, recognise that there's a pattern developing. Chances are, you're going into the room and employing some kind of short-term fix.

A PLAN: Nine times out of ten a child who wakes habitually doesn't need more food (unless she's going through a growth spurt; see page 55). Instead, reswaddle, if necessary give her a dummy to calm her, and comfort her with the shush-pat. Keep stimulation to a minimum. No rocking or jostling. Don't change her unless her nappy is soiled or soaking wet. Do the Four S routine and stay with her until she's settled into a deep sleep.

You also need to take steps to break the waking habit. So, let's say you've ruled out other causes such as pain or discomfort and you've eliminated hunger by upping her food during the day and tanking her up at night. Then I suggest my 'wake-to-sleep' technique (see box overleaf).

Breaking the bonds of trust. So many parents who come to me with sleep problems have tried this method or that, often co-sleeping or controlled crying. Inconsistency is a form of accidental parenting. It's not fair to keep changing the rules on your baby. And if you started out with your baby in your bed and then swung to the other extreme, you might also be dealing with a breach of trust.

Wake to Sleep? You've Got to be Kidding

You need to disrupt his pattern, so set your clock an hour earlier than your baby usually wakes. Jostle him gently, rub his belly a bit and stick a dummy in his mouth – all of which help stir him to semi-consciousness. He'll fall back to sleep. Do this for three nights in a row (if it doesn't work and his habitual waking is *definitely* not due to another cause, continue the technique for at least another three days). This gives *you* the control, rather than you sitting around hoping that your baby's habit will magically go away (it won't). Wake-to-sleep may be a shockingly counterintuitive suggestion, but it does work!

When a parent tells me that her baby 'doesn't like to go to sleep' or 'hates his cot', I always include the question, **Where has he been sleeping? A crib? A cot? In your bed?** When a child is resistant to the cot, it is almost always a case of the parent not starting as they meant to go on.

Did you subscribe to the idea of the 'family bed' when your baby was born? If 'yes', my hunch is that you didn't really think the philosophy through in practical terms, nor did you determine a timescale for moving him into his own crib or cot. If he's been in his own bed, and you're now taking him into your bed because it's more convenient in the middle of the night, you've definitely set up a pattern of accidental parenting.

I'm not an advocate of either

extreme. I don't believe that co-sleeping allows a child to develop the skills of independent sleep whereas, when we allow a child to cry alone, it can break the bond of trust between parent and child. Rather, I believe it's crucial to teach a child to sleep in his own bed, be it crib or cot, and encourage him to go to sleep on his own from Day One.

Have you ever left him to cry it out? I don't believe in allowing infants to cry alone, not even for five minutes. Trust is the foundation on which any relationship is built. Many babies who've been left to cry it out become chronically bad sleepers from that point on, even becoming fearful of their own beds. If you've tried one extreme and then swung to the other side, and now your baby is mistrustful and still not sleeping, you have to go back to Square One. Make sure you've got a good daily routine, and use the Four S wind-down ritual (pages 38–42). But please, please stick with it. There will be days and nights when things don't go as planned, and it may take three days, a week or a month to change a pattern. But if you follow my suggestions and are consistent, they will work.

Of course, the picture is more complicated if you've left your baby to cry it out, and he's now fearful about being abandoned. So you first have to build back the trust. Intervene and attend to his needs as soon as he makes a squeak – be *more* tuned in and *more* attentive to his needs than ever.

A PLAN: Be prepared to take several weeks to build back the trust, even if your baby is only three or four months old. (You'll find additional strategies for older babies and toddlers in later chapters, but the following can be used up to eight months.) Take slow, steady steps to show her that you're there – for good. Each step might take three days to a week until she trusts you enough to feel comfortable in her cot, and the whole process could take three weeks to a month.

Week 1: Keep a careful eye out for her sleep signals. At the first sign of sleepiness, begin the Four S wind-down ritual, including the shush-pat. Swaddle her and sit cross-legged with her on the floor with your back against the wall or a couch. When she is calm, lay her on a thick, firm standard-size sleeping pillow that sits on your knees. Continue the patting and shushing until you see her fall into a deep sleep. Wait at least 20 minutes more and then gently unfold your legs and let the pillow slide to the floor. Sit next to the pillow, so that you'll be right there when she wakes up. You must stay with her all night.

Week 2: Do the same routine but start with the pillow on the floor in front of you, not on your lap, and when she's ready, put her down on it. Again, stay by her side.

Week 3: Sit in a chair with her, and put the pillow in the cot. When you lay her on it, place your hand on her back (lay her slightly on her side so you have access to her back), so she knows you're still there. For three days, stand by her side until she's in a deep sleep. On the fourth day, remove your hand but stay by the cot while she's sleeping. Three days later, leave the room when she's in a deep sleep, but if she cries go back in *immediately*.

Week 4: You should be able to lay her down on her mattress, instead of the pillow. If not, use the pillow for another week and try again.

If it sounds tedious and a bit hard on you, it is. But if you don't take steps now to cure cot phobia, it will only get worse. Better to restore her faith in you *now*.

Variable Number 4: Hunger

Tip-offs

- My baby wakes up crying several times a night and has a full feed
- My baby doesn't sleep more than three or four hours at night
- My baby was sleeping five or six hours every night but suddenly started waking

When infants wake up in the middle of the night, it's often because of hunger. But that doesn't mean we can't do anything about it.

Tanking up. Whether your child wakes every hour or at least twice a night, I would ask you, **How often is he feeding in the day?** With the exception of premature babies (see page 35), feeds should be every three hours before the age of four months. If you're feeding less frequently, he is probably not getting enough food to sustain him and is waking at night to make up for the lost calories.

As your child grows, the goal is to extend the time between

night-time feeds to five or even six hours by first getting rid of the 2am feed. **What time does he wake up after his last evening feed?** If your child is six weeks or older – typically, old enough to miss one feed – and he's still waking at 1 or 2, he doesn't have enough calories to sustain him.

A PLAN: To encourage longer sleep at this point, make sure you feed your baby every three hours during the day. In addition, put a little more food in his tummy before bed by 'tanking up', which includes cluster feeding (giving extra feeds in the evening) and a dream feed (a 10 or 11 o'clock feed during which you try not to wake the baby).

Knowing – and responding to – the signs of hunger. You must always feed a hungry baby, but not every cry is a hungry one. Crying might indicate pain, or that your baby is overtired, or too hot or cold (see the Crying Questions on page 12). **What does he sound and look like when he's crying?** You'll know he's hungry (even before that first wail) because you'll see him lick his lips first and then start to root. His tongue will come out, and he'll turn his head like a baby bird looking for food. He might also flail his arms and try to hit what I call the 'feeding triangle' – which has the nose as its tip and the mouth as its bottom. Then he'll emit a vocal cue. You'll hear a kind of cough-like sound in the back of his throat and finally, the first cry, which is short to begin with and then a steady waa, waa, waa rhythm.

Of course, if your baby wakes up in the middle of the night crying, you don't have the benefit of the visual cues. But, if you listen carefully, with a little practice you'll hear the difference in his cries. If you're unsure, try a dummy first. If that soothes him, put him back into bed, swaddled. If he rejects the dummy, you know that it's hunger or pain.

Does she wake at different times every night? Erratic waking almost always indicates hunger. If you're not sure about the pattern, keep track for a few nights. But you also have to consider other questions.

Is he steadily gaining weight? This is a concern with babies after six weeks, especially if Mum is breastfeeding for the first time. Lack of weight gain could be a sign that the baby is not getting enough to eat, either because Mum's milk supply is still insufficient (it can take as long as the first six weeks for breast milk to be established) or because he's having trouble suckling.

A PLAN: If your baby is not gaining weight steadily, consult your doctor. If your baby is bobbing on and off the breast, you could have a slow let-down. If so, you need to 'prime' your breasts to get the milk flowing (use a breast pump for two minutes before you actually put your baby on your breast) or get a lactation consultation.

Growth spurts. You might have had your baby on a great routine. Still, at around six weeks, 12 weeks and at various intervals thereafter, your baby will probably go through growth spurts. His appetite will increase for a few days and, even if he's been sleeping five or six hours at a stretch, he'll suddenly start waking during the night for a feed, often every two to three hours, which is like a feeding schedule. Try upping your child's food during the day.

Often, if parents haven't recognised a growth spurt or they don't know what to do about it, they start feeding the baby at night, instead of upping his calories during the day. And when they start feeding at night, they set up a pattern of accidental parenting.

A PLAN: It's a matter of conscious parenting. Notice what your baby is consuming during the day and at night. If you're formula-feeding, and he's draining his bottle at each feed, give him more – but don't add another feed. Simply add extra formula to each of his daytime feeds. If you're breastfeeding, you have to send a message to your body to manufacture more milk. So, for three days, you have to take steps to increase your milk production (either by pumping extra an hour after each feed, or switching your baby back to the first breast when he's emptied the second).

Using a dummy. When parents tell me, 'My baby wants to feed all night,' I suspect that they're confusing hunger cues with a baby's instinctual need to suck. **Does your baby have a dummy?** A dummy helps to calm babies down. Very few babies become dummy-dependent, and in those cases I suggest that parents discontinue their use. However, in my experience, most babies suckle themselves to sleep, the dummy falls out, and they continue to sleep peacefully. I would never start a baby four months or older on a dummy if she hasn't ever had one but, with younger children, using a dummy when a baby wakes up early from a nap or during the middle of the night is also a good way to test whether your baby is actually hungry or just needs to suck.

Although I advise parents to start weaning babies off their dummy by around three or four months, or later (if you confine dummy use to the cot), babies under that age need the extra suckling time. It is their only form of self-soothing. When a baby is only allowed to suck on the bottle or breast, she either doesn't feed efficiently (she does that loose jaw sucking thing; she's just using the time to suckle) or is fed too often (she instinctively starts to suck when falling asleep and Mum mistakenly offers the bottle or breast, thinking she's hungry). Both are examples of how accidental parenting starts.

A PLAN: If your baby resists a dummy at first, keep trying the dummy during his waking hours, as well as different types, starting with ones that resemble your own nipples. Also, ensure you place the dummy in your child's mouth properly – position it so that it hits the roof of his mouth.

Variable Number 5: Overstimulation

Tip-offs

- My baby doesn't settle down to sleep easily
- My baby wakes frequently or sleeps fitfully, often crying at night
- My baby fights taking his afternoon nap
- My baby falls asleep but then suddenly jolts himself awake a few minutes later
- My baby resists going down for a nap, and when he does, he won't nap for more than half an hour or 40 minutes
- We just started a new play group, and my baby's started waking up in the night

An overstimulated or overtired baby can't fall asleep, tends to sleep fitfully when he does, and often can't stay asleep either. Therefore, one of the most critical keys to aiding a baby's sleep is to start your wind-down ritual as soon as you see his first yawn or first jerky movement (see Variable Number 2).

Nap problems. Daytime sleep patterns tell me a lot about whether overstimulation or overtiredness play a role in nighttime sleep problems. **Have his naps during the day got shorter, or have they always been less than 40 minutes?** If your baby always took short naps, he's not cranky during the day and he's sleeping well at night, that might just be his biorhythm. But if his napping pattern has changed, it often means he's overstimulated during the day and probably not getting a good night's rest either. Some babies, around eight to 16 weeks, might start taking 20- to 40-minute power naps. If a child is overstimulated, as he drops into a deep sleep after 20 or more minutes, that jolt of the body wakes him up. Often, parents accidentally reinforce the pattern by going in at once instead of letting him fall back to sleep on his own.

A PLAN: Look at what you're doing during the day, and especially in the afternoon. Try not to have too much company or do too many errands. And don't involve her in stimulating activities or be anywhere with too-bright colours before bed- or naptimes. Take more time with your wind-down ritual (pages 38–42), including the shush-pat – overstimulated babies often take twice as long to settle down and they jolt into sleep (sometimes that sudden start wakes them). Stay with her until you see that she's in a deep sleep.

Missing the window. **Do you frequently keep your baby up because you think he will sleep longer?** Once he's overtired, he not only won't stay asleep longer, he'll have a restless sleep and perhaps even wake prematurely.

A PLAN: Stick to your routine. Observe your baby's cues. Once in a while it's okay to veer from your routine, but know your child – some children are easily thrown. **Do you keep your baby up for company, or**

Build in Quiet Time

Parents nowadays are eager to make their children smarter, to make sure they know their colours and have watched every educational child's video on the market. No wonder children are overstimulated. The antidote is to build in quiet time for your infant. Encourage low-key activities during the day – staring at a mobile, cuddling with a person or a soft stuffed animal for a while. While you're at it, give her quiet time in her cot.

so that you and/or Dad can see him after work? I understand how hard it is for working parents to be separated from their baby during the day, but, if you keep your baby up later, chances are your time with him won't be particularly enjoyable because your baby will be overtired and out of sorts.

Developmental disturbances. Overstimulation is often caused by physical development. **Has your baby recently made physical advances – turning her head, finding her fingers, rolling over?** Often parents complain, 'I put my baby down in the centre of the cot, and a few hours later, he's crying. When I go in, he's all scrunched up in the corner.' Or 'My baby was sleeping fine until she started to roll over.' What happens is that, even if they swaddle her, she manages to wriggle out and roll from side to back. Then she can't roll back to her original position, and that might wake her and frustrate her. Also, because babies are totally uncoordinated at this age, they can wriggle a hand out of the swaddle, pull their ears and their hair, poke themselves in the eyes – and wonder who's doing it to them. They also start to realise that they can make little noises that both entertain and disturb them.

A PLAN: There will be periods when your baby's physical

development definitely stands in the way of sleep. Obviously, some of these changes you just have to ride out. Others are solved by swaddling. If rolling over is a frequent problem, use a wedge or rolled-up towels on either side of your baby's body to keep him stable.

Increased activities. As the day wears on, babies get more and more tired, just from regular activities like being changed and hearing the vacuum cleaner hum. **How much stimulation does your baby get during the day? Have you introduced more activities? If so, does she tend to have sleep disturbances on that particular day?** If a child seems to love a particular Mother and Child group or a music class, you may decide that a day's poor sleep is worth it. But, if an activity disturbs your child's sleep more than that one day, you probably should re-evaluate it.

A PLAN: If too much activity seems to affect your baby's sleep, don't go out after two and three in afternoon. If you can't avoid it – for example, you have an older child to pick up at 3.30, accept that the baby might fall asleep in the car and might not get a good nap. Or try to at least get her to take a 45-minute catnap in the late afternoon before dinner. It won't ruin her sleep; she'll sleep better for it.

Variable Number 6: Discomfort

Tip-offs

- My baby doesn't settle down to sleep easily
- My baby wakes up frequently at night
- My baby falls asleep but then wakes up within a few minutes
- My baby only falls asleep in an upright position, like the swing or car seat
- My baby seems tired, but the minute I start to put her down, she cries

It's obvious: babies cry when they're hungry and overtired, but also when they're in pain, uncomfortable (too hot or cold), or sick. The question is, which is it?

Looking for signs of discomfort. A structured routine enables you to make a better-educated guess about the cause of your child's crying. But you also have to use your powers of observation. **What does he sound and look like when he's crying?** If your baby grimaces, if his body gets rigid, if he pulls his legs up or flails wildly in his sleep or when trying to get to sleep, any and all of these signs might be indications of pain. A pain cry is more shrill and high pitched than hunger.

The important thing to remember is that at this age babies don't usually cry because of accidental parenting – it's because they need something. **Does he only fall asleep in his car seat, infant seat or swing?** One of the red flags of reflux is the baby who only sleeps in an upright position. The trouble is, they get used to an upright position and can't sleep any other way.

A PLAN: If you suspect that some type of intestinal pain is keeping your baby up or waking her, rather than encouraging swing addiction, or having to drive around or put her car seat in her cot, take steps to make her more comfortable in her own bed. Elevate the bed and any other surfaces you lay her on, like the changing table. Fold a receiving blanket in thirds, and wrap it around your baby's waist, like a cummerbund, and then use another blanket to swaddle her. The cummerbund's gentle pressure can ease the pain in a far safer way than putting your baby to sleep on her stomach, which parents of reflux babies are often tempted to do.

Constipation. Young babies have limited mobility so they tend to get constipated, which can disturb their sleep. **How many poos a day does she make? Is she formula-fed or breastfed?**

because 'normal' is different in formula-fed and breastfed babies. If a formula-fed baby goes for three days, she might be constipated. The problem doesn't happen as often with breastfed babies, who poo almost after every feed and then all of a sudden they don't poo for three or four days. That's normal. If a breastfed baby cries for no other apparent reason, is bringing his knees up to his chest and seems to be uncomfortable, he may be constipated, too. He might also have a distended tummy, eat less and/or have deeper yellow and more pungent urine, which might indicate that he's a bit dehydrated.

A PLAN: If your baby is formula-fed, make sure she gets at least 125 ml extra (4 extra ounces) of water a day or water mixed with prune juice (25 ml/1 ounce of prune juice to 85 ml/3 ounces of water). Give her 25 ml (an ounce) at a time, one hour after each feed. (Also be sure that you're mixing the right amount of water with the formula.) It can also help to bicycle her legs.

With breastfed babies, use the same remedy. However, you might want to wait a week to see if he's really constipated. If you're really concerned, see your doctor.

Wet discomfort. Before 12 weeks, most infants don't cry from being wet, especially if they're in disposable nappies that quickly absorb the moisture away. However, some infants are particularly sensitive and will wake if they feel wet.

A PLAN: Change her, reswaddle and calm her, and then put her back down. Use lots of nappy cream, especially at night, as a barrier against her urine burning her skin.

Thermal discomfort. **Do you feel his body when he wakes up – is he sweaty or clammy or cold?** The room may be too hot or too cold, especially when going from summer to winter. Feel his extremities. Put your hand over his nose and forehead. If it's cold, he's cold. **Is he very wet when he wakes up or soaked through?** Urine goes cold, and that can make his entire body cold. On the other hand, some babies overheat, even in winter. In the summer, some babies also get clammy hands, feet and head. They ball up their fists and curl their toes under.

A PLAN: Raise or lower the temperature of the room. If he's cold, swaddle him in a second blanket or a warmer one. Put an extra pair of socks under his sleep suit. If he regularly kicks out of his swaddle, try one of those fleece sleeper suits which stay nice and warm all night.

If your baby is warm or clammy, use a lighter receiving blanket (rather than an undershirt under his sleep suit). If that doesn't work, you might have to swaddle him naked with only his nappy on.

Using the Six Variables: What Comes First?

The six variables are not in any particular order. Indeed, more often than not, sleep disturbances are caused by at least two if not three or four of the variables – at which point parents ask, 'So what do I tackle *first*?'

Here are five common-sense guidelines to go by:

1. *No matter what other variables are at work and what other steps you have to take, keep or establish your routine and a consistent wind-down ritual.* In virtually every instance, I recommend doing the Four S ritual and staying with the child until he's in a deep sleep.

2. *Make changes in the day before you tackle night-time issues.* None of us is at our best in the middle of the night. Besides, making changes in the day often solves night-time problems without your having to do anything extra.

3. *Deal with the most urgent issue first.* Use your common sense. If, for example, your baby is in pain, no technique will work until her discomfort is relieved.

4. *Be a 'P.C.' parent.* You need **P**atience to effect change. Expect each step to take *at least* three days, or longer if the bond of trust has been broken. You need **C**onsciousness to hone your awareness of your baby's sleep signs and of his reactions to this new regime.

5. *Expect some regression.* This is very common (especially with little boys). Go back to Square One and start all over again. But please don't change the rules on your child.

Frequent problems

To help you see how these guidelines affect my thinking, I'm going to cover a series of the questions I often get asked and, with some, include extracts from emails or the telling phrases I often spot.

How Much Sleep Help Is Too Much?

Remember that in the early months we're teaching babies to go to sleep. Particularly if you've tried other methods, it can take weeks, even a month, to change a pattern or calm a baby who's become fearful. Sometimes parents get confused and wonder how much they should be doing.

> We are concerned that we are becoming a tool for Hailey to fall asleep during her naps. When should we stop trying to help her sleep? If she isn't crying, but still wide awake and fighting sleep, should we just walk away? What do we do when she starts crying again? It is hard to tell when our job ends and her job begins.

When a young baby needs help, we give it. Rather than worry about 'spoiling' her, we keep the focus on reading her cues and meeting her needs. In this case, the parents are not doing too much – in fact, they need to stay with Hailey to help her fall asleep. I suspect that trying 'cry it out' methods has compromised this baby's trust. Hailey sounds like a baby who needs to feel safe and needs extra calming down. Unless her parents stick with it now, taking the extra time during the day and before bed, they'll regret it in the months to come.

How Parents' Needs Can Overshadow the Baby's

Sometimes parents' self-interest, such as when they are about to go back to work, stands in the way of seeing the real issues.

This was the case for Sandor's mother. At 11 weeks little Sandor slept for seven and nine hours at a time. Sounds pretty good in my book. This mother's major concern was the fact that her son had 'reverted' to waking at 4am and disturbing her sleep. I suspect he was going through a growth spurt and waking out of hunger (he had already got to the point of sleeping long stretches so his tummy was big enough to hold an amount of food that could sustain him for seven hours). She has to up his calories during the day. If she starts feeding Sandor during the night instead, it will establish a habit and then she'll really have a problem on her hands.

Sandor's Mum was also upset that she was not seeing any changes after only four days. Sandor was almost three months old and, the older a baby is, the longer it takes to change bad habits. She needs to stick with one plan and ride it out.

Improper Intervention: No P.U./P.D. Before Three Months

Some parents who've read about my pick-up/put-down method (see chapter 3) try it on babies under three months, which is too stimulating for a young baby. Only the shush-pat is appropriate for calming infants. My suggestion is to spend time doing the Four S wind-down ritual and to remain in the room until the baby is fast asleep. Stand by the cot, pat him when his little eyes pop open again, and also shield his eyes with your hand to block out visual stimulation. I guarantee he'll go back to sleep and stay asleep. But each time the cycle is interrupted you'll have to start over again. Best to spend the time now!

First Things First

As I explained at the outset of this chapter, many sleep problems have multiple causes. We need to figure out what to do first. The following, from Maureen, is one for the books, as they say:

> Dylan has been a fussy sleeper for all seven weeks of his life. He started out with days and nights reversed. He has disliked sleeping in his crib from the start and this has got worse over time. He has cried for more than an hour in there and even when I try the pick him up, put him down method [see chapter 3], it didn't work. He startles himself awake after 5, 10, 15 minutes, if and when he does fall asleep, and then can't put himself back to

sleep. He wants to be held and cuddled most of the day and night and usually sleeps well then. Things are getting worse – I need to get Dylan on some sleep schedule but can never count on him taking a nap or staying asleep under any circumstances.

Throughout her email Maureen seems to attribute wilfulness to Dylan ('he fights', 'he wants', 'he dislikes'). She avoids taking responsibility for what she has done (or not done) to affect her son's behaviour.

Maureen's expectations are also a bit high. She says, 'He started out with days and nights reversed.' *All* babies start on a 24-hour clock, and if parents don't teach them to separate day from night (see pages 33–34), how will they know the difference? She points out that Dylan 'can't put himself back to sleep', but no one has taught him how! Instead, they've taught him that sleeping means being held and cuddled.

But the most telling part of Maureen's email is her revelation that Dylan 'has cried for more than an hour in there'. By leaving Dylan to cry on his own for so long, she has broken the bond of trust. No wonder he's now hard to console. The fact that Dylan regularly 'startles himself awake after 5, 10, 15 minutes' tells me that he is also overstimulated.

So where to start? It's clear that this mother has to commit to a structured routine – waking him every three hours in the day for a feed will deal with the day-for-night issue. But first she has to get him out of the crib, which is probably uncomfortable, and begin to build back the trust. She should begin with the pillow method (see pages 50–51) and very gradually move him to his cot. His parents have to do the Four S ritual – *at every sleep time, not just at night.* And each time, someone has to stay at Dylan's side until he's fast asleep.

The Vicious Circle of Reflux

I get countless emails from parents who say their babies 'never sleep' or are 'up constantly'. Some have already been diagnosed with reflux, but the parents are still having trouble making their babies comfortable enough to sleep. Others don't realise that their babies are in pain. In all of these cases, you have to deal with the pain first.

Firstly deal with the pain caused by his reflux by elevating all areas where you lay him (see pages 62–63). If you haven't already done so, seek the help of your doctor who can prescribe antacid and/or pain medication to relieve your baby's symptoms. If you even suspect a digestive problem, check with your doctor first, not as a last resort.

In particular with reflux babies, you have to be very careful not to comfort your baby past the point that he stops crying. It's a certain set-up for accidental parenting. Granted, certain types of props – a car seat, an infant seat, a parent's chest or a swing – comfort a reflux baby because they elevate the head, and I understand parents' desperate need to relieve their baby's discomfort, but if you use a prop, long after the pain of reflux disappears, the baby will still be dependent on it.

So this chapter has given you the information you need to be able to figure out what questions you might have to ask, and to put together various plans of action. I realise that this is a lot of information for you to absorb, but the better you are at assessing problems when your baby is three months old or younger, the better prepared you'll be for the rest of the baby and toddler years.

CHAPTER THREE

Pick Up/Put Down

A Sleep Training Tool – Four Months to a Year

When I met James, he was five months old and had never slept in his own cot. He couldn't sleep unless his mum was right next to him, in Mum and Dad's bed. But James's mum, Jackie, had to put herself to bed at eight o'clock every night and lie down with him every morning and afternoon when James took his naps; his poor dad, Mike, had to sneak in when he came home from work. And James *still* didn't sleep well. In fact, he woke several times a night, and the only way his mother could get him back to sleep was by breastfeeding him.

As with many babies who have sleep difficulties during the first year, the problem originated when James was only a month old. When he seemed to 'resist' their efforts to put him to sleep, his parents first took shifts in a rocking chair. He'd fall asleep eventually, but the moment they put James down, his eyes would pop open. In desperation, Mum started to calm him by laying him on her chest. Dead tired herself, she lay down in her own bed with him, and the two of them fell asleep. James never went into his own cot again. Each time James woke, Jackie would put him on her chest and hope that he'd fall back to sleep. She'd always end up giving him an extra feed as well.

This was a full-blown case of accidental parenting. I get literally thousands of calls and emails from parents of four-month-olds in many variations – and if parents don't take steps to change the situation, these types of issues get worse and last well into toddlerhood, if not longer. I picked James's case because it embodies all those problems!

By the time babies are three or four months old, they should be on a consistent routine and sleeping in their own cots for naps and night-time. They should also have the skills to settle down to sleep and to put themselves back to sleep when they wake up. And they should be sleeping through for at least a full six-hour stretch.

To determine how to solve a sleep problem, especially with older babies, we have to look at the entire day. Every issue can be traced back to an inconsistent, non-existent or inappropriate routine. Of course, some degree of accidental parenting is also involved. In every case, the solution involves getting the child back on to a good routine. To establish or tweak a routine with a baby three months and older, I teach parents 'pick up/put down' – P.U./P.D.

What Is P.U./P.D.?

Pick up/put down is both a teaching tool and a problem-solving method. With it, your child is neither dependent on you or a prop for going to sleep, nor is he abandoned. I use P.U./P.D. on babies from ages three months through a year – sometimes later, in particularly difficult cases or where a child has never had any kind of routine. P.U./P.D. doesn't replace the Four S wind-down ritual; it's more a measure of last resort. I use it to:

- teach prop-dependent babies how to get to sleep on their own, during the day and at night
- establish a routine in older babies or re-establish one
- help a baby make a transition from a three-hour to a four-hour routine
- extend too-short naps
- encourage a baby to sleep longer in the morning when early waking is due to something the parents have done, not the baby's natural biorhythms

P.U./P.D. is not magic. It involves lots of hard work. After all, you're changing the usual way you put your baby to sleep so she's probably going to cry because she doesn't comprehend what you're doing. Depending on how old and how physically strong and active your baby is, you will adapt the practice accordingly (see pages 80–102), but P.U./P.D. is basically this same simple procedure.

When the child cries, you first try to comfort him with words and a gentle hand on his back. Up to six months, you can also do the shush-pat; in older babies, the shush-pat – especially the sound – can actually disrupt sleep, so we just lay a hand on the child's back instead to make our presence felt. If he doesn't stop crying, then pick him up. But put him down the minute he stops crying and not a second later. If he cries and arches his back, put him down immediately, but maintain contact by placing a firm hand on his back so that he knows you're there. Stay with him. Intervene with words as well: 'It's just sleep time, darling. You're only going to sleep.' Even if he cries the minute he leaves your shoulder or on the way down to his cot, still lay him all the way down on the mattress. Then, if he's crying, pick him up again. In essence, your behaviour says to him, 'You can cry, but Mummy/Daddy's right here. I know that you're finding it hard to get back to sleep, but I'm here to help you.' On average, P.U./P.D. takes **20** minutes, but it can go on for an hour or more. I've had to do it over 100 times with some babies. Often, parents are sure it won't work with *their* baby. But you have the tools of your voice and the physical intervention, and you're letting your child know that you're not going to abandon him. Babies whose parents do P.U./P.D. eventually associate the voice with comforting, and they no longer need picking up to reassure them.

If you do P.U./P.D. correctly – pick her up when she cries and put her down the minute she stops – she will eventually lose steam, and cry less. At first, she might start snuffling, gasp in between whimpers, as she's winding down. Those short shallow breaths are almost always a sign that sleep is around the corner. Just keep your hand on her. The weight of your hand coupled with verbal reassurance lets her know you're there. You don't tap, you don't shush and you don't leave the room . . . until you see her drop into a deep sleep (see page 42).

P.U./P.D. doesn't prevent crying. But it does prevent fear of abandonment, because *you stay with the child and comfort him through his tears.* He's not crying because he hates you, or because you're hurting him. He's crying because he's frustrated. P.U./P.D. is about reassuring and instilling trust. If it takes 50 or 100 times, or even more, surely you're prepared to do that in order to teach your baby to sleep and to get your own time back, aren't you? There are no short, easy solutions.

To be effective, P.U./P.D. has to be developmentally appropriate. After all, dealing with a four-month-old is different from dealing with an 11-month-old. It makes sense, then, to adapt P.U./P.D. to fit baby's changing needs and characteristics. (As before, please read through all the age groupings.)

Three to Four Months: Tweaking the Routine

A baby's fourth month is the time when most babies are able to transition from a three- to a four-hour routine (see chapter 1). The four-month window also sometimes coincides with a growth spurt. However, unlike earlier growth spurts, this one not only involves giving more food during the day but also extending the time between feeds as your baby's tummy is now larger and he's a more efficient eater. He also needs more because his activity levels are about to increase, and he can stay up longer. This is the month when many sleep troubles develop.

At three months your baby is growing by leaps and bounds. He can move his head, arms and legs and might be able to roll over. He's more alert and tuned in to his environment.

A hungry baby, of course, always needs to be fed. But a tired and/or frustrated baby needs to be taught how to go back to sleep. He might arch his back as he's crying. If he's not swaddled, he also might throw his legs up in the air and slam them down on the mattress when he's frustrated.

Common issues. If a child has no structure in his life, or hasn't made the transition from a three- to a four-hour routine, there's a good chance he will either wake in the middle of the night, take only catnaps, wake up too early – or all of the above. Also at this age, just as a baby drifts into a deeper level of sleep, her body (and lips) go slack and the dummy pops out. While many babies stay asleep, some wake. For those babies, the dummy is a prop (see pages 56–57). If you keep popping the dummy back into your baby's mouth, you're reinforcing a common pattern of accidental parenting. Instead, just leave it out and comfort her in other ways. (If you haven't offered a dummy until now, it's best not to start.)

Key questions. **Have you ever had your baby on a routine?** If not, you'll have to introduce one (see chapter 1). **Are you trying to keep your baby on a three-hour routine?** If so, you've got to start helping him make the transition to a four-hour one. The process is the same as putting a four-month-old on E.A.S.Y. (see page 21). **Are his naps getting shorter?** This, too, could mean that your baby should be on a four-hour routine. At around four months or so, babies can start to hold their own for at least two hours and too-frequent feeds will cut into naptime. Even if they've been napping well up to this point, they then start to take shorter and shorter naps. Don't let the pattern get established. Instead, switch to a four-hour routine.

Does he want to eat more often – say, he's due for a feed at 10am but seems extremely hungry earlier? When he wakes at night does he take a full feed? If so, he's probably going through a growth spurt. Start moving him to a four-hour routine. Resist the temptation to feed him more often. Instead, gradually increase the amounts at each feed. By four or four and a half months (with the exception of a premature baby), he will be able to last four hours between feeds.

Does he wake up earlier? At this age, babies don't necessarily cry for food the moment they wake up. Many will babble and coo, and if no one goes in to them, they fall back to sleep. If your baby cries because he's hungry, you have to feed him. But then put him right back to sleep. If he doesn't fall asleep, do P.U./P.D. to get him there. As you increase his food intake during the day and move from a three- to four-hour routine, his wake-up time will probably stabilise. **In the past, have you always gone in to him and given him a feed?** If so, it's a pretty sure bet that he's got into a bad habit. Instead, do P.U./P.D.

How to adapt P.U./P.D. With a baby this young, you may have to reswaddle. Do it while he's lying in the cot. If you can't comfort him in his cot with reassuring words and a soft, reassuring pat, then pick him up. Hold him until he stops crying, but no more than four or five minutes. Don't keep holding him if he's fighting you, arching his back or pushing away from you. Try to use the shush-pat to calm him in the cot. If that doesn't work, pick him up again. On average, P.U./P.D. takes around 20 minutes to work at three or four months.

Early Wake-Ups
Your Baby's or Yours?

Babies have their own internal clocks. If your baby is getting 11½ hours of sleep – say from 6pm to 5.30am – that's the proper amount of sleep, especially if he naps well during the day. You could try to extend his bedtime, say to 6.30 or 7 – testing it out in 15-minute increments, to make sure he doesn't get overtired. But his body clock might resist, in which case you have to keep the 6 o'clock bedtime. If *you're* tired because you don't like getting up so early, go to sleep earlier!

Changing your four-month-old's day to solve sleep problems at night

When four-months (or older) babies are kept on a three-hour E.A.S.Y. routine, they have irregular naps and often wake at night. The following plan, designed specifically for a four-month-old, is given in three-day increments, and shows the timings clearly. Don't worry if your child takes more time to get to the goal.

Days One to Three. Watch your baby's three-hour routine, how much he eats, how long he sleeps. Typically, three-month-olds eat five meals a day at 7, 10, 1, 4 and 7.

Days Four to Seven. Feed your baby at 7 when he wakes up, extend his morning activity time by 15 minutes, and for the rest of the day his feeds will be 15 minutes later. He will still have three naps plus a catnap, but the span *between* naps will have increased a bit. Use P.U./P.D. to extend his naps.

Days Eight to Eleven. Continue feeding your baby at 7 when he wakes up, but extend his morning activity time by another 15 minutes. You will also eliminate his late afternoon catnap for a few days in order to extend the other three naps. Without the catnap, your child may be very tired in the afternoon; you might need to put him to bed at 6.30 instead of 7.30.

Days Twelve to Fifteen (or longer). Now extend your baby's morning activity time by *half an hour* more, which will make all his subsequent feeds half an hour later as well. Continue to avoid his late afternoon catnap (again, put him to bed earlier if necessary) to allow his other naps to lengthen. These will be the hardest days, but stay with it. If you've been cluster feeding, top him off at 7 before bed.

The Goal. At this point (see timeline on page 22), his morning feeds will be at the proper times – 7 and 11. Over the three days or week (or more), you work on adjusting the afternoon meal-times. Hold off for 15 to 30 minutes on the two afternoon feeds. As you extend his awake time, your baby will probably need his catnap. By continuing on this path you eventually consolidate the five feeds into four – at 7, 11, 3 and 7, plus the dream feed – and the three daytime sleep periods into two two-hour naps in the morning and early afternoon, plus a catnap in the late afternoon. You also increase his awake time so that your baby is staying up for two hours at a stretch.

If you're changing a child from a three-hour routine to a four-hour routine, or getting a four-month or older baby on E.A.S.Y. for the first time, these are the only times I suggest clock-watching. Especially when parents can't read their baby's cues, keeping close track of the time gives them an idea of what he needs. Extending your child's naps during the day, getting him back to sleep in the middle of the night and, if necessary, extending his morning wake-up is where P.U./P.D. comes in.

Four to Six Months: Dealing with Old Problems

As your baby's physical repertoire expands, mobility can cause sleep disturbances. She is starting to get up on her knees and can push herself forwards in the bed – you'll find her scrunched up in a corner of her cot. She might try to get up on her knees and lift her torso off the mattress when she's frustrated. When she's tired, her cry will reach three or even four very distinct, escalating crescendos: each time, the cry will start and get louder and louder and more and more frantic, and then all of a sudden it will reach a peak and start to come down the other side. If you're trying to correct accidental parenting or you've missed her cues and she's got overtired, you'll also see a lot of body language: when you hold her, she'll start to arch herself backwards or push down with her feet.

Common issues. Many problems are those we've seen in earlier stages, which haven't been dealt with. If movement wakes her and she hasn't developed the skills to put herself back to sleep, that could cause night waking, too. Sometimes parents are tempted either to introduce solids earlier or to put cereal into her bottle at this point but, contrary to myth, solid food doesn't make babies sleep any better. Too-short naps can be a problem too.

Key questions. The same as in earlier stages. **Has she always had short naps, or is this something that started recently?** If it's a recent occurrence, I ask about other issues – what's going on in the household, feeds, new people and activities (also see 'A Few Words on Naps', page 102). If things have been pretty stable, **Does your baby seem cranky and out of sorts after her nap? Does she sleep well at night?** If the baby is fine during the day, and a good sleeper at night, it might just be her biorhythm, but if she is cranky during the day, we have to do P.U./P.D. to extend her naptimes, because she obviously needs more sleep.

The Mantra Cry

The 'mantra cry' is an odd burst of a cry that most babies do as they're settling down. We *don't* pick up with a mantra cry. Instead, we hold back to see if the child can settle herself. We *do* pick up with a genuine cry, because it's your baby's way of saying, 'I have a need that has to be met.' The success of P.U./P.D. depends, in part, on your knowing the difference between a genuine cry and a mantra cry, which you should be able to do by the time your child is three or four months old. Each mantra cry is unique to the individual, but she'll do a kind of 'waa . . . waa . . . waa' sound. Like a mantra that's repeated over and over, the pitch and tone is the same throughout. It does *not* sound the same as a genuine cry, which usually escalates in volume.

How to adapt P.U./P.D. If your baby is burrowing her head into the mattress, turning her head from one side to the other, getting up on her knees, or flopping from side to side, don't pick her up right away. If you do, you'll get kicked in the chest or have your hair pulled. Instead, continue to talk to her in a low, reassuring tone. When you do pick her up, *hold her for only two or three minutes*. Put her down even if she's still crying. Then pick her up again, and follow the same routine. Babies at this age are more likely to put up a physical struggle when you're trying to change a habit; if your baby fights you, don't keep holding her. At that point, say, 'Okay, let me lay you down.' She probably won't stop crying, because she's in fighting mode. Pick her up straightaway. If she again starts to fight with you, put her in the cot. See if she can start to settle herself on her own and perhaps lapse into a mantra cry (see box opposite). Lay her on her back and hold her little hands and talk to her, 'Hey, hey, come on, shhh. You're just going to sleep. Hey, hey, it's okay. I know it's hard.'

Parents with babies around the five-month age range often comment, 'I've picked the baby up, and she calms down. But then, when I go to put her back down, she starts crying, before I've even got to the mattress. What do I do?' You lay her all the way down, take away the physical contact, and then say, 'I'm going to pick you up again.' Or else you're teaching her to cry in order to get picked up.

A common problem is that a parent holds the baby too long. It doesn't take very long for a baby to realise that *when I cry like this Mum or Dad come running*. And it doesn't take very long for them to associate going to sleep with being picked up. Now this may sound strange to you. My method is pick up/put down. The problem is, at this age in particular, many parents comfort past the baby's needs and the pick-up part is too drawn out.

Typically, something has happened to the child that affected her sleep, as in the case of Rona and six-month-old Sarah: 'We moved her from our room into her new room. The first two nights she slept well but now she wakes up. Oh, and I also started working part-time – Mondays through Wednesdays.'

That was a lot of change for a six-month-old. I thought it was best to explain the plan to both parents and Rona's mum, who would be with Sarah during the days that Rona was away from home.

Because Sarah was so accustomed to her mother intervening in the middle of the night, I suggested that Ed be the first to use P.U./P.D. when his daughter woke. He would do it on Friday night and Saturday, and Rona was not to go in to help him (if she thought she'd be tempted, I suggested she left the house altogether). She would be 'on duty' the next two nights.

The first night Ed had to pick Sarah up over 60 times before she'd settle, but he was also proud that he could finally get her down. The next night when Sarah woke, it took only 10 minutes to get her back to sleep. Sarah stirred on Sunday night but then put herself back to sleep. For the next three nights, Sarah slept all the way through. However, on Thursday night, she woke again. Because I had warned Rona and Ed that there might be a regression – there almost always is in cases of habitual waking – Rona at least knew what to expect. She went in to Sarah, but only had to do P.U./P.D. three times to get her to settle. Within a few weeks, Sarah's midnight waking was a distant memory.

Six to Eight Months: The Physical Baby

Your baby is much more physically advanced now. She is working towards independent sitting or is already sitting up on her own and may be able to pull herself to a standing position as well. She should be sleeping a good six- or seven-hour stretch through the night some time by the end of the fourth month, certainly by the time solid food is introduced. Dream feeds stop at around seven to eight months but it's important not to stop the dream feed abruptly; it can cause sleep problems if you do. So you must gradually increase the calories during the day before taking them away at night.

Common issues. Increasing physical abilities and motion can disturb a baby's sleep. When she wakes as a normal course of sleeping, she might sit up in bed if she doesn't go back to sleep immediately, or even stand up. If she hasn't yet mastered the art of getting down, she'll be frustrated and will call out to you. Your child also might experience tummy aches as solid foods are introduced (that's why you always introduce new foods in the morning). Teething has to be factored into the equation at this age, as well as booster shots, and some babies begin to experience separation anxiety as early as the seventh month as well (see 'Eight Months to a Year').

Key questions. **Does your baby get up at the same time every night or are his wake-ups random? Does he just wake up once or twice throughout the night? Does he cry? Do you immediately go in to him?** I've already explained that random waking usually means he's going through a growth spurt and/or is not getting enough food during the day to sustain him through the night (see pages 54–56). Habitual waking, on the other hand, is almost always a sign of accidental parenting. If he's just waking up once a night, try my wake-to-sleep technique (see page 48). If he is waking up *several* times a night, it's not just his body clock jarring him awake, it's also because, the minute he stirs, you've been rushing to his side. And if this has gone on for several months, you have to do P.U./P.D. to get him out of the habit. **Do you start the wind-down ritual the moment he gets tired?** By six months, you should know your baby's sleep cues. **Do you put him down the same way you always did? Was he**

always like this? What have you done to calm him in the past? If this is a new occurrence, ask yourself what his routine is like, what he does as activities, what changes have occurred. **Has he cut out a nap?** At this age, babies still need two naps, so he might not be getting enough sleep during the day. **Is he very active, able to move independently by scooting, crawling, pulling himself up to an upright position? What kinds of activities is he doing?** You may need to do calmer activities with him before sleep periods, certainly in the afternoon. **Have you started him on solid foods? Do you introduce new foods only in the morning?** New foods might be upsetting his tummy.

How to adapt P.U./P.D. Generally, when parents say, 'He gets more upset when I pick him up,' they're talking about a baby who's between six and eight months old. So instead of swooping down and picking him up, hold your arms out, and wait until he holds out his. Say, 'Come into [Mummy's/Daddy's] arms. Let me pick you up.' The minute you pick him up, put his body into a horizontal cradled position, and say, 'It's okay, we're just going to sleep.' Don't rock him. Put him down immediately. Don't make eye contact when comforting him – he can't help engaging with you if you do. You may have to help him control his flailing arms and legs: you could wrap a blanket tightly around everything but one arm. Holding him firmly but gently might help him settle.

Once he starts to calm, what you'll see is some self-soothing. The cry might be more of a 'mantra' cry (see page 88). Leave him alone, but be a soothing presence. Keep a gentle hand on him but don't shush or pat. At this age, the sound and sensation can keep a baby awake. If he cries again, extend your arms and wait for him to extend his. Continue the reassuring talk. If he raises his arms towards you, pick him up again and do the same thing. When he's settling, you might have to take a step back so he doesn't find you a distraction.

Shannon was at her wits' end about eight-month-old Kelly's night-time behaviour and, more recently, her naptimes too. 'Kelly screams like crazy when it's time to go to bed! She screams like this every time she falls asleep in her bed, in the car or in her pram. I know she's tired because she rubs her eyes and pulls at her ears. I keep her room dark. I've tried with and without a night-light, with music and without music . . . I just don't know what to do any more.'

Though Mum *thought* she hadn't done any accidental parenting, it was clear from what Shannon said that this had been going on since Kelly was born. Certainly, it's important to comfort a crying child, but Shannon was holding Kelly *too long*. Although I applauded Shannon for observing her daughter's sleep signs, by the time an eight-month-old rubs her eyes and pulls at her ears, she's pretty tired. Mum has to act earlier. On my advice, Shannon tried P.U./P.D. first at naptime and then at night. She called me the next day, 'Tracy, I did everything just like you said, but she was worse, just screaming her little head off.'

So we had to go to a Plan B, which is often necessary with an older child who has been in a bad sleep pattern since birth. When it was time for Kelly's nap, we did the customary wind-down ritual. Then I laid Kelly on the mattress. She started crying immediately so I put the side of her cot all the way down and climbed into the cot *with* her. I put my whole body into the cot. I put my cheek next to Kelly's. I didn't pick her up. I just used my voice and my presence to calm her. Even after she settled and drifted into a deep sleep, I stayed there. She woke an hour and a half later, and I was still at her side.

Shannon was confused: 'Isn't that co-sleeping?' I explained that the end goal was for Kelly to sleep independently. Also, I sensed she had a fear of her cot. Otherwise, why would she 'screech'? It was therefore important for me to be present when she woke up. Furthermore, we didn't take Kelly into an adult's bed. Rather, I stayed with her *in her own bed*.

When I delved deeper, Shannon admitted that she had tried the controlled crying method 'once or twice' over the last several months but gave it up because 'it never worked'. Each time Shannon had done a complete 180-degree turn on her daughter. She'd left her to cry it out, and then started to pick her up again.

In these kinds of cases, you can't even go to P.U./P.D. until you deal with the trust issue. For Kelly's second nap, I got into the cot *first* and asked Shannon to hand her baby to me. I lay down, and then when Kelly was lying next to me, I climbed out of the cot. Naturally, Kelly started to scream. 'Now, now,' I said to her in a soft reassuring voice. 'We aren't going to leave you. You're just going to sleep.' At first Kelly's crying was intense, but it only took 15 times of stroking her tummy to get her to sleep. Shannon continued P.U./P.D. that night when Kelly woke up. She realised that cradling Kelly in her arms and putting her down straightaway was very different from picking her up and holding her. I also encouraged her to put Kelly into her cot for increasingly longer periods just to play (see box opposite).

After a week, Kelly started to like playing in her cot. Her naps and night-time sleep became more consistent. She still woke every now and then and screamed for her mum, but at least Shannon now knew the proper way of doing P.U./P.D. and was able to get her baby to settle fairly quickly.

Eight Months to a Year: Accidental Parenting at Its Worst

Many babies are cruising, some walking, and all can pull themselves up to a standing position at this point. They often use toys in the cot as missiles when they can't sleep. Emotional life is richer, too – their memories are greater, and they understand cause and effect. At this age separation anxiety is usually full blown as they're old enough to realise that something is missing. Images from TV will also stick in their mind and can disturb sleep.

Making the Cot Fun

If your child has an aversion to her cot, put her in it when it's not time to sleep. Make it into a game. Put lots of fun toys in the cot (remember to take them out at bedtime, though). At first, stay in the room with her, putting clothes away, for example, but talk to her the whole time. As she becomes involved with her toys and begins to see that the cot is quite enjoyable and not a prison, you'll eventually be able to leave the room. Don't overdo it, though – and never leave her to cry.

Common issues. Because your baby has more energy you might be tempted to keep him up later. But at around seven or eight months, he'll actually want to go to bed earlier, especially if he's cut out a nap. Although teething, a more active social life and fears can cause occasional night waking, when the pattern persists it is almost always due to accidental parenting. Of course, if he's scared, you must comfort him; if teething, you must treat the pain – and in both cases offer a little extra cuddling. But you have to draw the line, too, so that you don't *overreact.* He'll pick up on your pity and will very quickly learn how to manipulate you.

This also can be an unstable time for the routine. Some days your baby might need a morning nap; on others, she'll skip it altogether or skip her afternoon nap. Most babies now take a 45-minute nap in the morning, and a longer one in the afternoon. Some will go from two one-and-a-half-hour naps to one three-hour nap. Don't panic – if you go with the flow, and remember that it will only last for a few weeks, you're less likely to indulge in accidental parenting.

Key questions. **How did the night waking happen, and what did you do the first time? Does he wake up at the same time every night?** If you can set a clock by him, it's almost always a bad habit. If erratic, and particularly if he is around the nine-month mark, his waking might be due to another growth spurt. **If this has been happening for several days, have you continued to do the same thing? Do you take him into your bed?** It only takes two or three days to develop a bad habit. **Do you offer him a bottle or breast when he wakes?** If he's drinking, it could be a growth spurt; if not, it's accidental parenting. **Does this only happen with you or with your partner as well?** Often, one person tells me that it's separation anxiety and the other doesn't agree. Clearly, it's best if parents can coordinate their efforts and each take charge every two nights as inconsistency will eventually lead to sleep problems. **Do you try to keep your baby up a little later now that he's older?** If so, you're breaking into the natural pattern you've established, which could upset his sleep. **Does he have teeth? How is his feeding?** Some babies teethe very badly and they can be miserable. They often start to refuse food, but then they wake in the night because they're hungry. If I suspect fears, I also ask, **Has he ever choked on solid food? Has something scared him recently? Has he started a new play group? If so, has anyone started to bully him? What's changed in your household – a new nanny, Mum going back to work,** a move to a new house? **Have you introduced any new things to watch on TV or video?** He's old enough to remember images that might later scare him. **Did you move him from cot to bed?** I think moving babies into a big-kid bed at a year is too early (see page 118).

How to adapt P.U./P.D. When she cries for you, go into her room, but *wait for her to stand up*. An eight- to twelve-month-old can often settle a lot more quickly out of your arms. So don't pick her all the way up, unless she's very upset. In fact, with most babies over ten months, I just do the P.D. part of the method. While standing at the side of the cot, put your arm underneath her knees, and with your other arm around her back, turn her and lay her back down on the mattress, so she's looking away from you, not at your face. Each time, wait until she stands up all the way before you lay her back down again. Then *immediately* lay her straight back down the same way. Reassure her with a firm hand on her back: 'It's okay, darling, you're just going to sleep.' At this age you start to use your voice even more, because they understand so much. Also start to name her emotions for her: 'I know you're [frustrated/scared/overtired].' She'll stand up again, and you may have to repeat the process many times. Use the same reassuring words and add, 'It's bedtime,' or 'It's naptime.' It's important to introduce those words to her vocabulary if you haven't already done so.

She'll eventually start to run out of steam. Then, instead of standing, she'll sit up. Each time, lay her back down. Remember that, at around eight months, she is starting to have enough memory recall to comprehend that, when you leave, you do return. So with P.U./P.D. your being there to comfort her is actually building that trust. It's also a good idea to tell her, at other points during the day, 'I'm going to the kitchen – I'll be right back.' It shows that you keep your word.

Frequently, parents of 10-, 11-, or 12-month-old babies, who have used P.U./P.D., will ask, 'My child has learned how to fall asleep on her own, but she cries if I don't stay until she falls completely asleep. So how do I get out of the room?' When you've done P.U./P.D. to the point of your child being able to settle fairly quickly, it still may take two or three days (or longer) for you to get out of the room. The first night, after she's settled down, stand by the cot. She will probably bob her head up to see if you're still there. If she is too distracted by your presence, stand first but then squat down to be out of her line of sight if possible. In any case, don't say anything and don't make eye contact. Stay there until you're sure she's in a deep sleep. The next night, do the same thing, but move further away from the cot. Each successive night, you keep moving back further towards the door until you're finally out of the room.

If your child suffers from separation anxiety, and starts clinging to you so you can't put her down, at least keep your body in the cot and reassure her, 'Okay, I'll stay right here.' When crying escalates, you pick her up again. Expect the crying to be fairly severe on the first night if you have previously tried a controlled crying method. In such cases, I bring in a blow-up bed and sleep in the child's room at least for the first night. On the second night I take the blow-up bed out, and only do P.U./P.D. Usually, by the third night, we're there (see also pages 126–127).

A Few Words on Naps

The issue of daytime sleep – children not taking naps, taking too short a nap, or napping erratically – cuts across all age groups. The complaint I hear most often from parents whose babies have nap issues is, 'My baby won't nap longer than 45 minutes.' No mystery there really. The human sleep cycle is approximately 45 minutes long. Some babies only make it through one sleep cycle, and instead of transitioning and going back to sleep, they wake up. (This sometimes happens at night, too.) They may make little baby noises or even let out a few mantra cries (see page 88). If a parent then rushes in, they become accustomed to taking these shorter naps.

Too-short naps, or no naps at all, also happens if a baby is overtired when he first goes to sleep (in which case he might not even last the full 40 minutes) or if parents wait too long to put their baby down. When he yawns, rubs his eyes, pulls at his ears, or maybe even scratches his face, his sleep window is already open. Act immediately. Overstimulation is a common cause of nap disturbance, so it's also important to get your baby *ready* for a nap, as you would at bedtime. You can't just plunk him in bed without a wind-down.

Poor napping habits are often part of an overall sleep problem, but we almost always work on naps first, because good daytime sleep leads to good night-time sleep. To lengthen naps, chart your baby's day for three days. (Six- to eight-month-olds also take a first nap at around 9. Between nine months and a year, the morning nap might be as late as 9.30. Regardless of age, however, the same principles apply to extending naps.)

There are two approaches you might take:

1. *Wake-to-sleep.* Instead of waiting for him to wake, go into his room after 30 minutes, because that's when he first starts to come out of a deep sleep. (Remember that sleep cycles are usually 40 minutes.) Before he comes all the way up to consciousness, gently pat him until you see his body relax again. It could take 15 or 20 minutes of gentle patting. If he starts to cry, though, you'll have to send him back to sleep with P.U./P.D.

2. *P.U./P.D.* If your baby is resistant to naps altogether, you can use P.U./P.D. to put him to sleep. Or, if he wakes up 40 minutes after you put him down, you can use the method to send him back to sleep. Granted, the first time you try this to remedy either situation, you might spend the entire nap period doing P.U./P.D., and then it's time for the next feed. Because sticking to the routine is as important as lengthening his nap, you need to feed him and then try to keep him up at least half an hour before putting him down for his next nap – at which point you'll probably have to do P.U./P.D. again because he's overtired.

Admittedly, tweaking naps can be a frustrating undertaking. In fact, it takes longer to establish a good nap schedule than it does to solve night-time sleep problems – typically, a week or two compared to a few days. That's because, during the day, you only have the span of time from when the nap begins to the next feed – usually around 90 minutes. But I promise that (unless you give up too soon or fall into any one of the following pitfalls), on the days that follow, P.U./P.D. will take less and less time, and your baby also will sleep for longer periods each time.

The Dirty Dozen: Twelve Reasons P.U./P.D. Won't Work

1. *Parents try P.U./P.D. when their baby is too young.* P.U./P.D. can overstimulate babies under three months.

2. *Parents don't understand why they're doing P.U./P.D. – and therefore do it wrong.* P.U./P.D. is to teach the skills of self-soothing when the shush-pat isn't enough. I never suggest starting off with P.U./P.D. Some parents also hold their baby for too long.

3. *Parents don't realise that they have to look at – and adjust – their baby's entire day.* You can't solve a sleep problem by just looking at sleep patterns or even by focusing on what's happening right before sleep time. You have to look at what your child is eating and especially at his activities. The calmer you can keep them, the better they'll be at sleeping.

4. *Parents haven't focused on their baby's cues and cries or how to watch her body language.* P.U./P.D. has to be tailored to your child. My timings are estimates. If your baby's breathing gets deeper and her body more relaxed in less time, put her down. Also, only pick up in response to a genuine cry, not a mantra cry (see page 88).

5. *Parents don't realise that as the baby develops they have to adapt P.U./P.D. to make it developmentally appropriate.* P.U./P.D. is not a one-size-fits-all technique.

6. *Parents' own emotions get in the way, especially guilt.* When they comfort their child, parents sometimes have a tone of pity in their voice. P.U./P.D. won't work if you sound as if you're feeling sorry for your child. A guilty parent (often one who feels they don't see their baby enough during the day) is often

unable to zero in on a particular strategy and stick with it – all of which can induce fear in a child. Parents who feel guilty are also more likely to give in.

7. *The room isn't ready for sleep.* You have to minimise distractions; P.U./P.D. rarely works in broad daylight or with the stereo blaring in the background.

8. *Parents don't take their child's temperament into consideration.* P.U./P.D. has to be tailored to different personality types. You just have to be prepared to do it a little longer with some babies. Also, the quieter the activity time before bed, the better it will go. You've got to build in at least 15 or 20 minutes of wind-down time.

9. *One parent isn't ready.* P.U./P.D. doesn't work unless both partners are on board. I can give parents all the plans in the world, but if they come up with a thousand reasons not to do it and keep insisting it will never work, then it won't work.

10. *The parents don't coordinate their efforts.* A good solution anticipates any unforeseen contingencies that might come up – a Plan B. At the same time, parents need to be aware of the

pitfalls when both of them do P.U./P.D., as shown in this email from five-month-old Trina's mum, Ashley:

> I am in the middle of trying P.U./P.D. This morning she didn't fall asleep at all. When I start to put her to sleep and then my husband comes in to give me a break, she cries hysterically whenever my husband picks her up, and then comes down when I take her. Is that normal?

This is a very common scenario: Mum gets tired and grumpy, and then Dad has to intervene. But, even if Dad steps in and starts doing P.U./P.D. exactly as Mum did, it's the same as starting over. It's a new person, and we all know that babies don't respond the same way with each parent. Also, when both parents are in the room it can be very distracting, especially if the baby is six months or older. Therefore, I usually suggest that each parent commit to taking two nights in a row so that the baby is only dealing with one parent at a time.

Mum also has to be careful not to try to take over in midstream: 'Even if that baby reaches out to you, you have to let Dad handle it. If not, you're going to turn him into the bad guy.' In the same vein, Dad has to commit to staying the course. He can't, in the midst of his baby's cries, turn to his wife and say, 'You do it.'

11. *Parents have unrealistic expectations*. I can't repeat this too many times: P.U./P.D. is not magic. It doesn't 'cure' colic or reflux or ease the pain of teething or make an obstinate baby easier to handle. She will be very frustrated when you start – expect a lot of crying – and with all situations and all temperaments you have to allow time for change and expect a relapse.

Your baby might not conform exactly, but the following four most common patterns will give you an idea of what to expect:

- If a child goes down reasonably fast with P.U./P.D. – say within 20 minutes to half an hour – you'll probably get a three-hour window out of her at night. So if you start at 7, that first night you'll be doing P.U./P.D. at 11.30 and then again at around 5 or 5.30am.

- If you have a child who is eight months or older and has been waking frequently at night for several months, and you've responded with some form of accidental parenting, you might have to do P.U./P.D. over a hundred times. And he's not going to sleep more than two hours the first time around. Be prepared to do it again and again and again for the first few nights.

- If a child has been taking short naps – anywhere from 20 to 45 minutes apiece – when you first start to do P.U./P.D., she typically will stay asleep only for 20 minutes more because she's not used to sleeping longer than 45 minutes. Go back in and do P.U./P.D. until you get her back to sleep, or until her next feed period, whichever comes first. But never allow her to sleep past her feed time.

- If you've done the controlled crying method and left your child to cry it out, P.U./P.D. will take longer (naps or night-time) because your child is fearful. Sometimes you'll have to take steps to rebuild the trust before you can even attempt it. P.U./P.D. does eventually work, and when it does, you might have two or three nights of full sleep. Then, on the third night, he wakes up. But that only means you have to be consistent and do it again.

12. *Parents get discouraged – and then don't stick with it.* When they have a bad night or a bad day, many parents feel as if P.U./P.D. has failed them. It hasn't, but if you quit now it will. Even if your baby sleeps 10 minutes longer than he used to, that's progress. Believe me, I recognise that P.U./P.D. is both difficult and trying for parents. So I'm not surprised when . . .

They cave in as early as the first night. When I later ask, **How long did you do it?** they say, 'Ten or 15 minutes, and then I couldn't stand it.' For babies with deeply entrenched problems, I've done it for over an hour. Believe me, the second time gets shorter.

They try it for a night and stop. If you've been consistent with accidental parenting, you have to be just as consistent with strategies meant to correct the situation.

They give up after they've had just a little progress. Say they've gone from a 20- or 30-minute nap to an hour nap. Mum is happy with the hour, but that's not enough to keep her child on a four-

---

P.U./P.D. Survival Strategies:
How NOT to Give Up

☑ P.U./P.D. is very stressful for one parent to do alone. Even if you don't have a partner, a parent or a best friend you can team up with, at least invite someone over for moral support. It will be helpful for you just to have someone there for *you*.

☑ Start P.U./P.D. on a Friday, so that you have the weekend and are more likely to secure the above-mentioned help.

☑ Use ear plugs when you're in the room with the child. This is simply to deaden the sound of her crying a bit, so it's less likely to grate on your ears.

☑ Don't feel sorry for your child. You're doing P.U./P.D. to help her become an independent sleeper, which is a great gift.

☑ If you're tempted to quit, ask yourself, 'What will the situation be if I cave in?' You'll be right back where you started.

hour routine. Staying the course avoids a return of the problem later on.

They experience initial success but when the problem recurs, as sleep issues often do, they don't go back to P.U./P.D. They try something else instead. If they had stayed with P.U./P.D. it would have taken less time to get back on track because the baby will remember.

Of course, there are no pat formulas for dealing with sleep problems, but I've personally never had a case in which P.U./P.D. didn't work. Remember that if you are as consistent with the new method as you were with the old, it *will* eventually produce change. Keep in mind also that at this point sleep problems are infinitely more manageable than if you let them slide into toddlerhood. That might be the best incentive of all!

CHAPTER FOUR

'We're Still Not Getting Enough Sleep'

Sleep Problems after the First Year

A Sleep Crisis

According to a poll conducted by the American National Sleep Foundation babies and toddlers (which they define as 12 to 35 months) aren't getting enough sleep.

- *Sleep problems are persistent well past infancy.* Sixty-three per cent of toddlers experience sleep-related problems, and almost half of toddlers wake at least once a night.

- *Most babies and toddlers go to bed too late.* Nearly half of toddlers are in bed after 9pm (I recommend a 7 or 7.30pm bedtime at least until age five).

- *Many parents are in denial about their children's sleep habits.* Around a third of parents with toddlers said their children were getting less sleep than they should. But when asked, on another question, whether their child gets too little, too much, or the right amount of sleep, 85 per cent said that their child gets the right amount of sleep.

- *Accidental parenting is alive and well among parents of toddlers.* Close to half of all toddlers go to sleep with a parent in the room, and one in four is already asleep when put to bed.

The good news is that the poll also shows that parents who teach their child the skills of independent sleep tend to have children who sleep better. For example, children who are put to bed awake are more likely to sleep longer than children who are put in bed already asleep (9.9 hours compared to 8.8 hours) and nearly three times less likely to wake repeatedly during the night (13 per cent versus 37 per cent).

This was the largest study to date to examine the sleep habits of young children, and it shows that a whopping 69 per cent of young children experience sleep-related problems a few times a week.

Sleep Issues in the Second Year

Developmental changes and a growing sense of independence account for some sleep problems in the second year. **Is he walking? Is he talking?** Even late walkers have significant leg strength by now. This new-found physical achievement can affect him when he's resting as well – in particular during the period in which he is taking those first few tentative steps. Some children stand themselves up in the middle of the night while still sleeping and walk around the crib. Then they wake up, don't know how they got there, and don't know how to get down. Also, muscle spasms can wake your child and so can the sensation of falling.

I don't recommend allowing young toddlers to watch TV or videos, because these media can overstimulate or leave disturbing images in their little heads, which also can upset their sleep. At one year, REM time decreases to about 35 per cent, but there is still ample time for dreaming in a young toddler's sleep. You also need to consider the rest of the family. **Has he got older siblings who wind him up?** When a toddler starts to walk, it becomes fun for his brother or sister to torment him – all in good fun, of course. But this can really upset a child and also cause him to wake up at night.

Your young toddler is more inquisitive as well as active. Even if she's not talking in full sentences, she is probably chattering more and certainly understands everything you say. You might hear her in the morning babbling to her stuffed animals – unless you run right in, this developmental achievement gives you a few more delicious moments in bed.

When a formerly good sleeper suddenly starts having sleep problems as a young toddler, I also look for clues related to his health or in his environment. **Have you changed the household routine? Is your child teething? Have you started new activities? Has he been sick recently? Have you started a new play group? Have there been changes in the lives of other family members with regard to work, health, availability?** You may have to think back several weeks or months, and look at what happened and what you did in response to it. Naps get trickier now, too. This is a time when children usually transition from two one-and-a-half- or two-hour naps to one long one. That seems simple enough on paper, but the getting there can be full of ups and downs. Your toddler might skip his morning nap for a few days, but then revert to his old pattern for no apparent reason. And, unlike younger babies for whom good naps ensure a good night's sleep, I often warn parents to get the child up by 3.30 so there is enough activity time for him to expel his energy and get ready to sleep. That said, if your child has lost sleep in previous days and needs to catch up, or if he's sick and needs more sleep than activity time, then by all means allow him to sleep a bit later.

The most important developmental leap is the fact that your child now understands cause and effect, which means that accidental parenting can happen a lot faster. Each lesson you teach (consciously or not) is put into that little computer, and stored for future uploads. Let's say your 15-month-old wakes up suddenly at 3am If you rush in, pick her up, and say to yourself, 'Just this one time I'll read her a book to calm her down,' I guarantee that tomorrow night she'll wake up and want you to read her a book again, and she'll probably up the ante as well, demanding two books, a drink and an extra cuddle. That's because she's able now to actually make the connection between what she does and what you do.

It's not hard to tell when a parent has fallen into this trap. **Does he have tantrums during the day?** Once a toddler learns how to manipulate, the behaviour colours his whole day. Two key questions help me determine whether a child has a troubled history when it comes to sleep: **has your child ever** slept through the night? And **have you always had trouble putting him to bed?** A 'no' to the first question and 'yes' to the second tells me I am looking at a child who has never learned to fall asleep on his own and who lacks the skills to put himself back to sleep when he wakes. Then I find out what kind of props the parent has been using. **How do you put him down now? Where does he sleep? Are you still breastfeeding? If so, do you use that as a form of putting him to sleep? Do you feel sorry for him when he cries at night? Do you rush in? Do you bring him into your bed? When he was younger, were you able to leave the room before he was fully asleep? How long are his naps in the day and where? Did you ever try the controlled crying method?** All of these kinds of questions also help me gauge the degree of accidental parenting.

Making the Cot-to-Bed Switch

Don't rush into it (try to wait until your child is at least two), but also, don't wait too long to make this transition if you're expecting another child. Start the process at least three months before the baby is due.

Do talk about the transition and involve your child in the process: 'I think it's time we got you a bed like Mummy and Daddy's. Would you like to pick out some new sheets for it?' If she's under two, consider a bed with removable sides to start with.

Don't change bedtime rules or your routine when you make the switch. It's more important than ever to be consistent.

Do send your child back to bed immediately – and without cuddling – if he manages to get out and comes into your room.

Don't feel guilty for enforcing a stay-in-your-room rule after bedtime and putting up a gate if necessary. If your child is an early riser and now comes into your room early in the morning, get him his own alarm clock or put a light on a timer – when the alarm goes off or the light goes on, he can come out.

Do make her room safe – cover outlets, get cords out of the way, put locks on lower drawers, so she can't use them for climbing to high places.

Don't take chances, especially if your child is under three. Place the bed against the wall; use a mattress only (no box spring), so the bed is closer to the ground; and, at least in the first few months, use a guard rail.

Sleep Issues in the Third Year

Many of the second-year issues continue into the third year, but older toddlers are more affected by changes in the family and in the environment. They're even more curious than their younger counterparts and noise can wake your child where it didn't before.

They are physically more able, too. **Does your toddler climb out of her cot and come into your room?** Some toddlers manage this feat as early as 18 months, and before the age of two your child's head is still out of proportion to her body so, when she leans over the cot side, she could topple over and fall out. But by two she might figure out how to climb over on purpose. And then she comes wandering into your room in the middle of the night. This is an age when parents normally start thinking about getting their child into a bed (see above). I say put it off as long as possible – at least until age two if not longer – because it somewhat curtails those middle-of-the-night visits. (The only exception is when a child is cot phobic; see pages 47–51.) **What do you do when your child comes into your room in the middle of the night?** If you allow it once or twice in a week, chances are you'll have a problem on your hands.

Because older toddlers are also extremely sensitive to changes in the household, I always ask, **Has life in your family changed?** A new arrival, parents' marital problems and/or divorce, new partners, a new caregiver, more challenging social situations – any of these can throw off an older toddler's sleep, especially if he's never learned to sleep on his own or to self-soothe. **Have you started a new play group** or added another type of group, like Mother and Baby, baby yoga, baby aerobics? Delve deeply and look at specifics, too: what's actually happening in the play group? What kinds of activities is your child being asked to do? What are the other children like? Even a child who was once a good sleeper can fall apart in the face of too much stress and, in particular, if he's the brunt of teasing or bullying.

Sleep problems are now more exhausting than ever for parents. These children have the gift of speech, to ask for a glass of water, just one more cuddle, and to endlessly negotiate and harangue. If it's a deeply entrenched habit, and the parent doesn't respond the way the child expects and wants, she's likely to get angry and shake the cot. She might have tantrums during the day as well.

Has your child ever slept through the night? In lots of cases we have to start at Square One. We have to look at emotional history as well, and for demanding behaviour: head-banging, pushing, slapping, biting, hair-pulling, kicking, throwing themselves on floor, going rigid when being held. Parents often mistake older toddlers' manipulation for separation anxiety, which nine times out of ten, if parents are gentle and reassuring and haven't resorted to some sort of accidental parenting as a solution to their child's fears, disappears by 15 to 18 months. Make no mistake, however: there are also genuine fears at this age, because comprehension is so much greater. Your child grasps fully what's going on around him: that one kid in play group always grabs his toys; that the little fish in *Finding Nemo* is separated from his daddy.

Because parents tend to allow more TV-watching and computer games in the third year, it's not surprising that nightmares go with the territory. It's important to try to screen everything you offer your child and see it through your child's eyes. Are you sure they'll really enjoy watching *Bambi*? Or might it be disturbing for a little child to see that the main character's mother is killed? Watch what kinds of stories you tell and books you read. Spooky tales and dark images might stay with your child. Most importantly, if television and computers are a part of your child's day, be sure to build in a wind-down time before bed.

Sleep Strategies for Toddlers

Many of the practices and strategies for younger babies are applicable to toddler sleep problems, albeit with some modifications.

Problem: Suddenly cranky during his bedtime routine
Plan: You still need a routine, but you might have to modify it as your child gets older

Lola called about her 19-month-old: 'Carlos is suddenly cranky during his bedtime routine. And he used to love his bath, but now he gets really upset.' After a few questions, it came out that the family had recently taken a trip to Lola's native Guatemala and also Carlos had started a new music class. I explained that she had to expect some reverberation. Additionally, because Carlos is more active now, his bedtime might have to move earlier. Also, at this age a bath before bedtime can overstimulate some children, in which case Lola would have to either bathe him earlier – say at 4 or 5 before dinner – or do a morning bath and quick sponge before bed at night. Lola protested at first: 'But we do the bath at night so Dad can do it.' Luckily, Carlos was adaptable and Lola was creative. She suggested that Dad try taking him into the shower in the morning. Carlos loved it, and a new ritual with Dad began.

Problem: Takes a long time to fall asleep; naps are inconsistent
Plan: Take pains to make your bedtime ritual consistent

Bedtime routines should of course include time for book reading and cuddling. In addition, because toddlers' comprehension is so much greater, you might consider adding conversation to the routine – this will help her process her day and settle at night. If you are tuned in to your child, it helps you design a ritual that really fits.

Problem: Having bad dreams
Plan: Use your bedtime ritual to anticipate problems
Two-year-old Olivia had been having bad dreams. So I suggested that when Dad put her to sleep he make a big deal about the furry little fox Olivia had adopted as her special comfort item: 'Don't worry, Liv. Googie will be here for you if you need him.' Figure out what will work with your child. The goal is to plant the idea that your child has the skills to see herself through the night. If incorporating other actions into bedtime rituals helps your child feel safe, like checking under the bed for monsters, by all means add that, too. And even before your toddler is fully verbal, going over the day is also a wonderful idea, because it helps a child process her fears.

Problem: Cries out at night
Plan: When your child cries during a sleep period, don't
             rush in
It's absolutely critical during toddlerhood to continue a

practice (I hope) you started when your baby was a wee thing: observe before you jump in. If your child doesn't cry, don't go into her room. If she does cry, try to distinguish whether it's her mantra cry or a genuine call for help (see page 88). If the former, wait a bit. If the latter, go in but say nothing. Don't talk to her; don't engage at all.

Problem: Wants to be rocked to sleep; can't get back to sleep on his own
Plan: 'P.U./P.D.' turns into 'P.D.'
Because toddlers are heavier than babies and harder to lift, and because you've lowered the mattress, I suggest just doing the put-down part (see page 100).

Of course this technique will take longer with children who've had a history of accidental parenting. Betsy, for example, wrote to me fully aware of what she'd done wrong with Noah:

> I've 'accidental parented' Noah so that he wants to be rocked as he sleeps. Some nights we hear him barking and talking and then he goes back to sleep on his own. But other times he wakes up crying. Now if he wakes up it's impossible to get him back in his cot! The minute I move to get up out of the chair, he begins to cry. He does the same thing at naptime. He's been doing this for, oh, around 18 months. Any suggestions?

This is obviously an old problem, which has never been resolved and then further complicated by toddler issues. Betsy and her hubby have *taught* Noah: *when I cry, they come running, and they rock me.* By now, Noah is consciously manipulating them. So here we need a two-part plan: put Noah into his cot without rocking, and, if he starts to cry, use P.D. They should stay in the room to show him that they're physically there for him, but they shouldn't talk to him. Under no circumstances should they pick Noah up. They should say comforting words. In fact, even though this has been going on for 18 months, Betsy might be surprised if she is really firm in her resolve.

Problem: Won't let me leave the room
Plan: If it's necessary to re-establish trust, stay with your child on a blow-up bed – even before you do the P.D. method

I can't say this often enough: a baby who has been traumatised by abandonment often has more severe sleep problems at this age, and solutions take longer. With tough cases I bring in a blow-up bed and sleep in the child's room at least for the first night. Put the bed next to the cot to start. If this is a recent sleep problem, you might be able to take the bed out after the first night. But if it's a very long-term problem, move the blow-up progressively further from the cot (and closer to the door) every three nights.

Each case is a little different. Sometimes I also do a transition step with a chair once I've got the blow-up bed out of the room. I sit in a chair positioned next to the cot as the child is falling asleep. I leave the room when he's sleeping. The next few nights, I move the chair further and further away.

If your toddler hasn't ever slept in his cot and/or is terrified of his cot, skip the cot and start making the transition to big-kid bed. Include him in shopping for the bedding and allow him to help you make the bed that afternoon. You will start by sleeping in his room with him on the first night on a blow-up mattress on the floor next to his bed. Then you gradually move your blow-up out, and sit in a chair for a few nights until he's asleep. If he comes into your room in the middle of the night, gently, and without any conversation, put him back into his bed. If it's a chronic problem, buy a gate and stress that he has to stay in *his* bed.

Problem: Comes into my room in the middle of the night
Plan: Always go to your child – don't allow her to climb into your bed

When she pays a call, take her right back to her own room. Be firm during the daytime as well. Make it a house rule that your toddler has to knock on your door. Model this yourself when you go into her room. It's about respect and boundaries.

Of course, in most cases, a child's middle-of-the-night visits don't come out of left field. For example, when I received this email from Sandra, I knew it wasn't the whole story:

> Elliott does not sleep by himself at night. We literally have to lie down with him on his queen-size mattress, which is on the floor. He seems to wake every couple of hours and gets mad and comes in and gets us to crawl back in bed with him. HELP! Truthfully, I don't know how much of the crying we could listen to because he was colicky for four months and cried around the clock. How do we get out of this cycle and get him to sleep alone?

First of all, why is Elliott on a queen-size mattress on the floor? I bet someone used to sleep with him. Since they've already been sleeping in his room, they should go right to the chair phase. At bedtime, they should bring in a chair and explain, 'Mummy [or Daddy – whoever is less likely to cave in!] will stay here until you fall asleep.' After three days, before going into Elliott's room to start the bedtime ritual, they should move the chair a foot closer to the door, so that Elliott doesn't see them doing it. Every three nights, the chair gets closer to the door. And each night whoever sits with Elliott reassures him, 'I'm still sitting in the chair.' When they're ready to move it, they tell him, 'Tonight we're going to take out the chair, but I'll stay here until you're asleep.' They'll keep that promise, standing a few feet away from him without engaging. Once the chair is out of the door, he hopefully will be able to settle down on his own. If not, when he tries to get out of bed or wakes up later in the evening, they have to take him right back to his room, with no eye contact or conversation, and without allowing Elliott to manipulate them. Eventually, they should take away the words, just do P.D. and lay him back in the bed. They have to make a commitment.

Problem: Afraid this will go on for ever
Plan: If your child was a 'bad sleeper' as a baby, it's important to analyse and respect your child's history, but don't let fear dominate your actions today

Read between the lines of Sandra's email (above); pay particular attention to these words: 'Truthfully, I don't know how much of the crying we could listen to because he was colicky for four months and cried around the clock.' It's obvious to me that Sandra is still recovering from Elliott's first four months and, now he's 18 months, they're petrified: will this go on for ever? Such anxiety about the past can sabotage any solutions we might come up with in the present.

Problem: Wakes up too early; gets tired by mid-morning
Plan: Use my wake-to-sleep technique to extend sleep times
Wake-to-sleep (see page 48) works well with toddlers, too. I often suggest it to parents who are dealing with either early morning wake-ups or habitual waking in the middle of the night. In some cases, in fact, wake-to-sleep is the first step of a plan. For example, Karen, mother of 17-month-old Megan, wanted to know how she could help Megan go from two naps to one. But when she told me that Megan was also up at six every morning, I knew we had to deal with that problem first. Otherwise, she wouldn't have the stamina to last until noon or 1pm, and she'd be too overtired to take a good long nap. I suggested that Karen go into Megan's room an hour earlier and wake her at 5am, change Megan's nappy and put her right back to bed, explaining, 'It's too early to start our day. Let's go back to sleep.'

Problem: Want to trim two naps a day into one
Plan: Make changes gradually

Sometimes parents come up with good plans on their own, but they also move too quickly without giving the child a chance to adjust to the new routine. For example, Karen had originally been trying to cut Megan's morning nap out all together and hoping she would just then take one long nap in the afternoon. Instead, she got overtired, ended up napping in the morning anyway or falling asleep in the car, and then slept fitfully. Instead of going cold turkey, Karen had to phase out her morning nap in increments.

Once Megan started to sleep a bit later in the morning, Karen could try to stretch her from 9.30 to 10, or if that was too much, just to 9.45. Then, three days later, she'd again extend the nap, using the same 15- or 30-minute interval. She could have a morning snack and then wake and have her lunch. The process took a month or so, and there were several days in which she regressed altogether – waking too early, taking a long morning nap. This was normal.

Problem: We caved in after one night
Plan: Be as consistent in the new way as you were in the old
When you do something differently your child will resist. If you stay at it and project an air of confidence and determination, you'll be amazed at the change. But if you're

half-hearted, your child will up the ante – scream louder, wake more often – and you'll cave in.

Problem: Grumpy after napping
Plan: Don't get confused between comforting your
              toddler and 'spoiling' him

Toddlerhood is an especially erratic time, and children need their parents' reassurance more than ever. One day he'll skip a morning nap; the next day he won't be able to make it through the morning. Besides, there's a lot of new stuff happening in the toddler's universe, but toddlers still need to know that Mum and Dad are there to comfort them when the going gets rough.

> Roberto is nearly two, and ever since I can remember, after he has had his daytime nap, he is really irritable and will scream and whine for an hour, and then just suddenly click out of it and be fine. If I sit by him, he will put his arms up to be held but then fight to be put down again. He will say he is thirsty but then refuse a drink, as though he's not quite sure what to do with himself. I've tried leaving him to wake on his own and ignore it, but that doesn't work either. He lies on his front with his arms and legs tucked under him, and normally sleeps for at least two to three hours. If he is woken he is even worse, and if someone comes into the house or makes a noise when he's like this he is even worse, too. He is fine when he wakes in the morning. Has anyone ever come across this before?

All humans have different wake-up patterns. In addition, Roberto is a very typical toddler. It is important to comfort him. Comforting your child is different from spoiling; it gives a child a sense of security. Roberto's mum needs to allow him his time to come back to consciousness after naps, rather than try to force him before he's ready. She could hold him for a little while and say, 'You're just waking up. Mummy's here. We'll go downstairs when you're ready.' My hunch is that Mum may be rushing him; if she gives him the time he needs, Roberto will probably just sit there for a few minutes. Then all of a sudden he'll notice a toy and reach for it. Or he'll just look up at Mum and smile, as if to say, 'Oh, I've come round now.'

Problem: Can't get her out of our bed; tried everything; still doesn't sleep through the night

Plan: If your child is having sleep problems in her second or third year, examine your own agenda – and what you've been doing until now

Some parents hate to let go of the baby years, and they comfort excessively and take their child into their own beds out of their needs, not the little one's. So ask yourself, **Are you really ready to allow your child to grow up? To have his or her independence?** This may sound silly but giving children freedom and teaching independence doesn't start when they're old enough to get a driving licence. You have to carefully plant the seeds now, balancing increasing responsibilities with love and nurturing. Remember, too, that children who sleep well have less tendency to cling, whine and act out during their waking hours.

Also, parents who have been doing accidental parenting or adopted a particular practice, like the family bed, often have a change of heart when their child becomes a toddler. They may be contemplating a second child or Mum is planning to go back to work, but here's the catch: just because you need a good night's sleep, it doesn't mean your baby is ready, especially if you haven't taken the appropriate steps to get him there.

> I feel I have done everything possible to help Edward sleep through the night and self-soothe, and now I have run out of ideas. We have a very good routine with him at bedtime and he goes to sleep on his own without crying 99 per cent of the time. We NEVER cuddle him to sleep, and I have never fed him to sleep either. He does not use a dummy, and has a special object 'Moo'.
>
> He wakes, and always has done at various intervals during the night and cries for us. We usually wait a while to see if he nods

back off, which sometimes he does alone. More often than not, though, he starts getting really agitated, so one of us will go in, we don't talk to him, we check that he is lying down, and that he has Moo. Harry and I give him a small sip of water from his beaker and then leave the room, at which point he will often go back to sleep. This doesn't sound like any big deal, but I work part-time and have prep to do at home in the evenings after he has gone to bed, I find it really hard when my sleep is disturbed at least twice a night, sometimes more and then often I can't get back to sleep again either.

When we try not going in at all, he ends up covered in snot from all the crying, standing up in his cot and too hysterical to comfort himself back to sleep.

Claudia has done a lot of the right things: established a good bedtime routine, avoided the feeding-to-sleep trap, and given her son a security object. But she has also misread some of my advice. Rocking a baby to sleep is not the same as cuddling him. Claudia also doesn't realise that she has, despite her good intentions, done some accidental parenting: she or Harry give Edward water every time he wakes. That glass of water has become his prop. But the most telling part of this email is the last paragraph: 'When we try not going in at all . . .' In other words, on more than one occasion, Mum and Dad have left Edward to cry it out. When he wakes up he not only doesn't know how to send himself back to sleep, he also doesn't know whether or not his parents will go in.

Where do we start? First of all, Claudia and Harry have to rebuild the trust. I would put one of them on a blow-up bed to be there when Edward wakes and to help him go back to sleep (see pages 126–127). They also have to get him out of the water habit – they can build this into his pre-bedtime routine by giving him a nonspillable trainer cup and explaining that he can find this on his own if he's thirsty.

Problem: Wakes up and wanders; often wants to climb into our bed

Plan: Help your child to spend time alone and to know when he can come out of his room

Marlene was crying when she first called about Adam. 'It's a nightmare . . . he refuses to sleep on his own and wakes up two or three times a night and then wanders . . . Even though I stick to my guns,' Marlene explained, 'it's a battle of wits all the time and this makes it very hard for my husband and me to cope. He is so strong-willed and tries to dominate. Like if he's playing, and I want to step out of the room, he goes ballistic. Isn't this late for separation anxiety? It's hard to keep our sanity sometimes.'

I knew right off that this wasn't so much a battle of wills as the result of two years of escalating accidental parenting. They had tried various methods, changing the rules on Adam. Now he is manipulating them.

They had also tried controlled crying with Adam, which was why he, at two, was so insistent on keeping his mum nearby at all times. This was clearly a case in which the trust had to be rebuilt before any other problems could be examined. We put a blow-up bed in his room and, for the first three days, Marlene went to sleep when Adam did. By the fourth night, after Adam fell asleep, Marlene left. A few hours later, he woke, so she went right in and stayed there until morning. The next night he slept through.

During the first week I explained to Marlene that she also had to be especially attentive to Adam, showing him that he could count on her to be there for him during his waking hours. She would say to him, 'Let's go into your room and play.' Once he was engaged with a toy or activity, she then very casually announced, 'I'm going to go to the bathroom.' The first day, he protested, but Marlene had a timer in her pocket. 'Mum's going to come back when the timer goes off,' she told him. Two minutes later, she returned to a tense but smiling Adam.

By the beginning of the second week, when Adam played in his room, Marlene was able to leave for five minutes. It was also time to take the blow-up bed out of Adam's room. That night they did the usual bedtime ritual but explained, 'I'm going to sit with you for a while when we turn the lights off. But when the timer goes off I'm going to leave.' They only set the timer for three minutes (an eternity to a child), so that Adam wouldn't be just drifting off to sleep and be awakened by the timer when it rang.

Not surprisingly, he tested his parents that first night, crying out the moment Dad shut the door. Dad went straight back in – and set the timer again. 'I'll sit with you a few minutes and then I'm going to leave.' This happened several other times. Once Adam realised that crying wasn't getting his usual result, he quietly got out of bed and came into the living room. Dad marched him straight back into his room without saying a word. They did this for two hours the first night. The second night, it happened only once.

Although what we really wanted was to stop Adam from marching into Mum and Dad's bedroom at 6am, we first had to get Adam used to the notion of staying in his room until it was time to come out. Marlene and Jack made a game out of it at first: 'Let's see if you can stay in your room until the timer alarm goes off.' When he did it successfully, they gave him a gold star. When he had five gold stars, they took him to a park where he'd never been before as a 'reward'.

Finally, they said to their son that he was ready for a 'big-boy clock'. They made a ritual out of presenting him with his first digital Mickey Mouse clock, showing him how the big '7' came up in the morning. 'When the alarm goes off like this, that means it's time to get up and you can come out of your room.' But here's the most important part of this strategy: although they set Adam's alarm for 7am, they set their own for 6.30. The first morning, they were outside his door when the alarm went off, and they went right in. 'What a good job – staying in your own bed until the alarm went off. That definitely deserves a star!' The next morning, they did the same thing. Finally, on the third morning, they waited to see what Adam would do. Sure enough, he didn't come out until the alarm went off and, when he did, they once again lavished him with praise.

Adam did not become magically more cooperative. He was still manipulative and tested his parents, but now at least his parents were taking the lead, instead of following their child.

I've often seen parents who settle for less than the original goal – for example continuing to co-sleep – either because they don't want to make the extra effort, because they can't imagine that a strategy will actually work, or because they have a genuine change of heart. Maybe it is for all three reasons. Who are we to judge why parents make a particular decision? In fact, I always say to clients, 'If it's working, that's fine – it's *your* family.'

Index

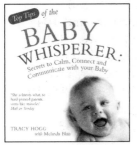

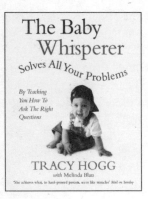